Date Due

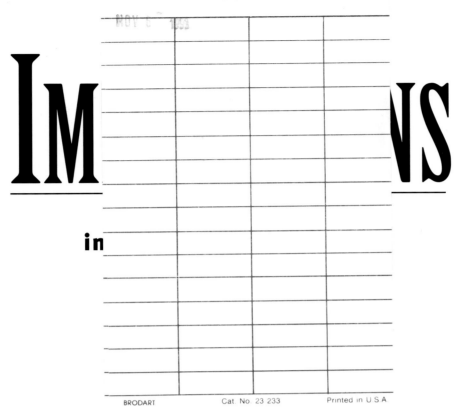

IM **NS**

in

Impressions: 250 Years of Printing in the Lives of Canadians
© **Her Majesty the Queen in Right of Canada, 1999.**

Published by Fitzhenry & Whiteside and the National Library of Canada
in cooperation with the Department of Public Works and Government Services.

Catalogue Number: SN3-325/1999E

Published in conjunction with an exhibition held at the National Library of Canada from April 24, 1999 to January 7, 2000
Author: Michel Brisebois

Canadian Cataloguing in Publication Data

Main entry under title:
Impressions : 250 years of printing in the lives of Canadians
Catalogue of an exhibition held at the National Library of Canada,
Apr. 1999 – Jan. 2000
Issued also in French under title: Impressions : 250 ans d'imprimerie dans la vie des Canadien(ne)s

ISBN 1-55041-408-9

1. Publishers and publishing - Canada - History - Exhibitions.
2. National Library of Canada - Exhibitions. I Brisebois, Michel. II. National Library of Canada. III. Title: Impressions : 250 years of printing in the lives of Canadians

Z483.I46 1999   070.5'097107471384   C99-930921-8

ACKNOWLEDGMENTS

Exhibition coordinator: Randall Ware

Exhibition curator: Michel Brisebois

Marketing and Publishing:
Margo Wiper, *Director*
Rhonda Wilson, *English-language editor*
Pierre Ostiguy, *French-language editor*
Dale Simmons, *Marketing*

Conceptual Design of Exhibition: Manon Tissot

Design and Development of Web Version: Andy Coughlin

Exhibition mounts: Kevin Joynt

Framing: Robert Lamoureux, Brian Schorlemer

With the help of the following curators:
Barbara Norman of the Music Division
Cheryl Jaffee of the Jacob M. Lowy Collection
Sandra Burrows of the Newspaper Collection

Editor: Rhonda Wilson

Design: Darrell McCalla

CONTENTS

Foreword	3
Introduction	4
Children's Literature and Education	5
Immigration and Transportation	13
Household and Family	20
Agriculture and Trades	26
Judicial and Political	32
Newspapers and Magazines	39
Leisure and Literature	42
Religion	52
Health	57
Book-Object	61
References Consulted	63
Appendices	63
Index	64

Foreword

It is with pleasure and pride that I welcome you to the National Library of Canada's world, one part of which is depicted in this catalogue of a major exhibition, "Impressions: 250 Years of Printing in the Lives of Canadians". Exhibitions such as this play an important role in that they enable Canadians to appreciate the depth and diversity of the National Library's comprehensive collection of Canadian publications. As well, the National Library's interpretation of the material shows the many and varied ways in which print has affected and continues to affect our lives.

Even as we embrace the latest technologies and speculate as to the future of the printed word, we would do well to remember that print is still the definitive record of our past. Libraries, such as ours, collect and preserve our published heritage. This precious heritage will always be central to the understanding of our country and ourselves.

I would like to take this opportunity to thank the staff of the National Library of Canada, and in particular Michel Brisebois, Rare Book Librarian, and Randall Ware, Public Programs Coordinator, who worked with such dedication to bring this exhibition to life.

This catalogue, like the materials it describes, is meant to inform, to educate, and to expand our awareness and appreciation of Canada's rich published heritage. May you find it both enjoyable and informative.

Marianne Scott
National Librarian

Introduction

During the last decade of the 20th century, the ever increasing use of the Internet as a source of information and communication has prompted some to predict the disappearance of the printed word. This exhibition is meant neither as a eulogy of printing, nor as a retrospective look at a form of communication about to be replaced, but rather as a reminder that printing in Canada, since its beginning in Halifax in 1751, has played a major role in the lives of Canadians, and that it will continue doing so.

In the past, exhibitions on the history of printing have taken many forms. Some concentrated on particular themes or periods of time, while others emphasized technological developments. Aesthetic and documentary qualities of illustrations, first productions of early colonial printers and libraries of well-known collectors have all been the subject of exhibitions.

Of all the reasons to own a book, the main one is certainly to use it, either as a reference tool or for its literary qualities. This exhibition shows two aspects of the printed word: the tool of learning and the communication of public information. The first concerns books people owned, used, read and re-read, wrote in, and often passed on to their children or friends. The book became an heirloom. The second concerns the printed object posted for public reading, and which contained timely information designed to be shared by many: the broadside.

Throughout this period, great quantities of books were imported from Europe and the United States through local book dealers or privately. Before Confederation, it was often more profitable for book dealers to import books than to print them. Nevertheless, the books displayed here show that printing in Canada was healthy and its products diverse.

To attempt to summarize the role of printing in the lives of Canadians in a single exhibition is, to say the least, an ambitious undertaking. Limits had to be set, and certain categories of printed objects, worthy of an exhibition of their own, restricted to representative examples. Popular literature was given limited attention, although there are a few books of this type in the Leisure and Literature section. From the second half of the 19th century, newspapers were the most widely read printed material in the country. Only selected examples, designed to show how news travelled, have been included.

The majority of the items exhibited were printed during the 19th century. The purpose is to show the period in which the greatest diversity and change occurred: the beginning of the transformation from colonial printing to mass-market publishing. Obviously the explosive changes in all types of publications which took place during this century could not be adequately reflected in the allocated space.

An attempt has been made to link the items shown to major changes in the economic, political and social life of Canadians. From 1791 to 1850, the population of British North America increased tenfold, mainly due to immigration from the United States and the British Isles. The political structure changed from one involving isolated colonial entities to one of representative government. After 1850, there occurred a gradual shift from a colonial to a continental economy, creating a need for improved transportation by water, by train, and later, by air. The development of manufacturing and retailing – and its corollary, advertising – and the mechanization of agriculture affected printing during the second half of the 19th century. A public system of education was established, and took over from the private system designed mainly for the upper classes. All these changes had an impact on print and its use.

The items shown are grouped by themes, and the themes, in turn, arranged in a loose chronological sequence reflecting a person's lifetime. The first part of the exhibition contains children's storybooks and textbooks, followed by immigration and transportation literature. This section is designed to represent the beginning of learning for those already in the country, the first glimpse of Canada by the immigrant families, and the tools useful to move about in their new land.

From city directories to trade catalogues, from appeals to women voters to emigration manuals, from rules of the courts to rules of baseball, the second section, by far the largest, shows the role of printing in the home, at work, and at play. These are the printed words used and read in adult life.

The third, and last, section contains items related to religion and health: pre-occupations of a lifetime but increasingly so as the years pass by. A final exhibition case is devoted to the book as an object – cherished, modified, personalized, and, in some cases, saved from destruction.

All the items exhibited are from the collections of the National Library of Canada. An effort was made to record and, in some cases, to identify previous owners of these books, to connect the user and the tool. This exhibition is not only about books; it is, in fact, about people.

Children's Literature and Education

Before one can use books, one has to learn to read. Most of the children's literature available to early Canadians was designed to moralize or instruct. Readers and other textbooks were crucial to the development of Canadian society. Before the 1850s, education was a private matter with the Church playing a major role. Textbooks were either imported, reprinted locally, or written by educators teaching in large religious institutions – certainly a captive market. During the second half of the 19th century, with the establishment of a public school system of education, the curriculum was standardized, teachers received training, and schooling, supported by taxation, became compulsory. The great demand for standardized textbooks across the country brought about the reprinting of series of schoolbooks from Ireland and Scotland. Large Canadian publishers such as John Lovell and James Campbell also published their own series. By the end of the century, Canadian educators were writing their own readers, grammars, and other school texts.

1 The Snow Drop.

1

The Snow Drop; or, Juvenile Magazine. 1847-1853.

Montreal: Lovell and Gibson; Toronto: Scobie and Balfour, and others.

The first successful children's magazine in Canada.

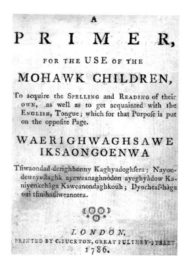

2 A Primer for the Use of the Mohawk Children.

2

A Primer for the Use of the Mohawk Children... / Waerighwaghsawe Iksaongoenwa...

London, England: Printed by C. Buckton, 1786. 98 p.

This primer was printed for Daniel Claus (1727-1787), deputy superintendent of Indians in Canada. A first edition had been printed at Fleury Mesplet's shop in Montreal in 1781. It was much used by the Loyalist Mohawks to study their own language, as well as English. The frontispiece, engraved by James Peachey, represents a class of Native schoolchildren receiving instruction.

5

3

Le Livre des enfans.

Québec: Thomas Cary et Cie., 1834. 24 p.

3 Le Livre des enfans.

4

JAKOB TEUSCHER

ABC Buchstabir - und Lesebüchlein, mit Rücksicht auf die Lautirmethode...

[ABC: Speller and reader: also touching on pronunciation...]. Berlin, C[anada] W[est] [Kitchener, Ont.]: Bödecker und Stübing, 1863. 45 p.

This German speller and reader was the sixth edition, stereotyped in Philadelphia. The plates were probably sent to Berlin (Ontario) and other German settlements to be printed.

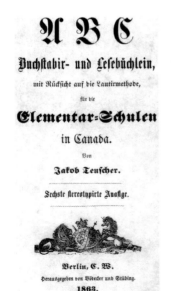

4 ABC Buchstabir - und Lesebüchlein.

5

I. FIGLER

Figler's Jewish Writing Method.

Montreal: I. Figler, [circa 1917].

A first book for learning to write Yiddish. Figler also published other books for learning to write Hebrew.

6

Little Folks Alphabet.

Toronto: Canada Games Co., [© 1919]. [10] p.

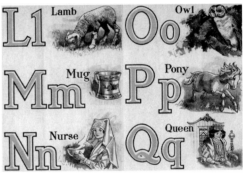

6 Little Folks Alphabet. (See colour insert p. i).

7

MAXINE [PSEUDONYM OF MARIE-CAROLINE-ALEXANDRA BOUCHETTE, 1874-1957]
ABC des petits canadiens... illustrations de J.-Arthur Lemay.

Montréal: Éditions A. Lévesque, 1933. 31 p.

Little Red Riding Hood

The original version of Little Red Riding Hood was written by Charles Perrault. In this version, the young girl and the grandmother are eaten by the wolf. The French-language versions, including those published in Canada, retained this tragic ending. In the English-language version, the one by the Brothers Grimm, the young girl and the grandmother are saved and the bad wolf is killed. This was the version used in English Canada. It is interesting to observe that the same fairy tale was essentially different for the children brought up in one or the other language.

8   *Le Petit Chaperon Rouge.*
(See colour insert p. i).

8

CHARLES PERRAULT, 1628-1703 AND EUGÈNE ACHARD, 1884-1976

Le Petit Chaperon Rouge: conte de Charles Perrault; adaptation par Eugène Achard; dessins de Roland Boulanger.

Montréal: Librairie générale canadienne, [circa 1940]. 24 p.

9

CHARLES PERRAULT, 1628-1703

Le Petit Chaperon rouge; Le Chat botté; Barbe Bleue; Riquet à la Houppe; et, Peau d'Âne...

illustrations de Gendron. 6e édition.

Québec: L.-A. Belisle, 1953. 61 p.

10

Little Red Riding Hood.

Toronto: James Campbell & Son, n.d. [between 1865 and 1884]. 6 leaves.

From a series of books called: New Series of Oil-coloured Toys.

11

NANCY KNIGHT

Little Red Riding Hood. Verses by Nancy Knight; illustrations by H.E.M. Sellen.

Toronto: Heaton Publishing, [circa 1900]. [16] p.

12

Little Red Ridinghood Illustrated by Primrose. A Television Book of Little Red Riding Hood.

Toronto: S. Lowe, c1951. [24] p.

Edition dating back to the beginning of television.

13

Little Red Riding Hood.

Fredericton, N.B.: Brunswick Press, [1954]. [15] p.

14

MARTHE FARIBAULT, 1952-

Le Petit Chaperon rouge. Illustrations de Mireille Levert; texte français de Marthe Faribault.

Saint-Lambert, Québec: Héritage, c1995. [30] p.

15*

MIREILLE LEVERT

Little Red Riding Hood.

Toronto: Groundwood Books, 1996. [29] p.

* This item is not included in the exhibition.

10   *Little Red Riding Hood. (See colour insert p. i).*

11   *Little Red Riding Hood. (See colour insert p. i).*

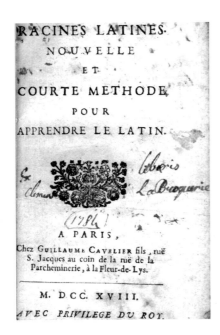

16 *Racines latines: Nouvelle et courte methode pour apprendre le latin.*

16

Racines latines: Nouvelle et courte methode pour apprendre le latin.

Paris: Chez Guillaume Cavelier fils..., 1718. [4], 108 p.

At the end of the 18th century, the majority of schoolbooks were imported from France or England. This Latin school text, printed in Paris 75 years earlier, was used at the Collège de Montréal in 1784 by Clément-Amable de la Broquerie (1772-1826), future parish priest of Lanoraie (1798-1804), and first parish priest of Rigaud (1804-1826).

17

JOSEPH FRANÇOIS PERRAULT, 1753-1844

Tableau alphabétique de mots de trois syllabes, à l'usage des écoles élémentaires Françoises.

Québec: C. Le François, 1830. 60 p.

The pioneer in secular education in French Canada, Perrault founded in Quebec City a school for boys and one for girls. Both schools operated with some difficulty from 1830 to 1837. A fervent Catholic but a champion of religious freedom, Perrault accepted Catholics and Protestants alike, and took charge of poor children who could not pay. In 1832, with Amury Girod, a recent immigrant from Switzerland, Perrault organized a model farm at Petite-Rivière-Saint-Charles near Quebec. Practical and theoretical teaching of agriculture was complemented with courses in languages, mathematics and the sciences. This ambitious project came to an end the following year because of a lack of students; the parents unable to pay the relatively high boarding costs. The school texts written by Perrault were used in many schools in Lower Canada for many generations.

One of the school texts used in Perrault's schools for boys and girls.

18

JOSEPH FRANÇOIS PERRAULT, 1753-1844

Traité d'agriculture pratique. Seconde partie; de la grande et moyenne culture adaptée au climat du Bas-Canada...à l'usage des établissemens d'éducation dans les campagnes.

Québec: Fréchette et Cie., 1831. 156, vii p.

Probably one of the school texts used in the courses at his model farm.

17 *Tableau alphabétique de mots de trois syllabes, à l'usage des écoles élémentaires Françoises.*

19
JOSEPH FRANÇOIS PERRAULT, 1753-1844

Code rural à l'usage des habitants tant anciens que nouveaux du Bas-Canada, concernant leurs devoirs religieux et civils, d'après les loix en force dans le pays.

Québec: Imprimerie de Fréchette et Cie., 1832. 31, iii p.

Perrault believed that farmers needed to have not only knowledge in agricultural matters, but also a minimum of information on the legal and judicial systems to allow them to protect their farms and have them prosper.

20
JÉRÔME DEMERS, 1774-1853

Institutiones philosophicae ad usum studiosae juventutis.

Quebeci: Ex typis T. Cary, 1835. 395 p.

This work is based on the lecture notes which Father Demers gave to his students during his philosophy course at the Petit Séminaire de Québec. Since schoolbooks were rare, it was the tradition among teachers to give lecture notes which students copied. Demers was of the opinion that to have a printed text would save time and would allow the students to concentrate on the subject. Copy belonging to Narcisse-Henri-Edouard Faucher de Saint-Maurice (1844-1897), one of the most prolific writers and journalists of 19th-century French Canada.

21
JEAN HOLMES, 1799-1852

Nouvel Abrégé de géographie moderne: Suivi d'un appendice, et d'un abrégé de géographie sacrée, à l'usage de la jeunesse.

Quatrième édition revue et augmentée. Québec: William Neilson, 1846. xiv, 322, [47] p.

The most popular geography school text in French Canada. It was used with a number of additions for more than 50 years. American-born and originally Protestant, Father Holmes was one of the great Canadian educators of his time. With Father Demers, at the Petit Séminaire de Québec, he taught history, geography and philosophy. He also took an active part in the training of teachers at the École normale de Québec. The statistical tables for Canada shown here were an innovation at the time.

22
JEAN BAPTISTE MEILLEUR, 1796-1878

Nouvelle Grammaire anglaise rédigée d'après les meilleurs auteurs.

St. Charles, village Debartzch [i.e. Saint-Charles-sur-Richelieu, Quebec]: Imprimé par A.C. Fortin, 1833. 120 p.

At first a teacher and an educator, Jean Baptiste Meilleur, one of the leading figures in education in French Canada, was superintendent of public education in Lower Canada from 1842 to 1855.

23
LINDLEY MURRAY, 1745-1826

The English Reader; or, Pieces in Prose and Verse, from the Best Writers: Designed to Assist Young Persons to Read with Propriety and Effect; Improve Their Language and Sentiments; and to Inculcate the Most Important Principles of Piety and Virtue.

Toronto, U[pper] C[anada]: Published by R. Lesslie & Sons, 1835. 251 p.

Stereotyping was done by making a mould from the face of a type form and filling it with molten metal. The resulting plate could be stored, copied or sent to numerous small printers. For this reader, the stereotyping was done by H.H. Wallis in New York, and the plates sent to Toronto where it was printed. The cost reduction for the printer was substantial.

24
D. MCMULLEN, PROPRIETOR

Picton Academies for Ladies and Gentlemen: The Summer Session of These Institutions Will Open on the Sixth of June, the Winter Session on the Seventeenth of October.

[Picton, Ont.: Picton Gazette Print, 1850].

This advertisement for a private school lists tuition fees and other expenses, such as fuel and candles. The students were expected to supply their own beds, bedding and towels.

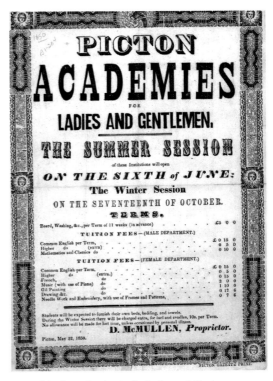

24 *Picton Academies for Ladies and Gentlemen.*

25
WILLIAM EUSEBIUS ANDREWS, 1773-1837

The Catholic School Book: Containing Easy and Familiar Lessons for the Instruction of Youth of Both Sexes in the English Language and the Paths of True Religion and Virtue. The 1st Montreal ed.

Montreal: Printed by N. Mower, 1817. 180 p.

Readers were often used to give religious instruction. Copy belonging to "Olivier Harel, Classe de Syntaxe, Petit Séminaire de Montréal, 1862-63," a surprisingly late use for this schoolbook.

26
STEPHEN RANDALL, ED. 1804-1841

The Canadian Reader: Designed for the Use of Schools and Families.

Stanstead, L[ower] C[anada]: Printed by Walton & Gaylord, for the publisher, 1834. 308 p.

American-born Stephen Randall was a schoolteacher in Upper and Lower Canada, as well as a journalist and reformer. This is an early example of Canadian editing of a literary anthology. In his preface, Randall stresses the fact that the children should understand, not simply read, the texts.

27
WILLIAM CHARLES ST. JOHN, 1807-1873

A Catechism of the History of Newfoundland: From the Earliest Accounts to the Close of the Year 1834 for the Use of Schools.

St. John's [Nfld.]: J. M'Coubrey, printer, 1835. 55 p.

The word "catechism" was used to describe the question and answer approach of this history book. This copy belonged to Henry Lind (1805-1870), a lay missionary of the Newfoundland School Society, and schoolmaster at Port de Grave on Conception Bay. Ordained in 1841, he was transferred to a large mission at Heart's Content on Trinity Bay. The copy later found its way into the collection of Dr. Robert Bell (1841-1917) of Montreal.

28
E.A. LEQUIEN

Grammaire élémentaire: À la portée de toutes les personnes qui n'ont aucune notion des principes de la langue française. Huitième édition.

Québec: Impr. de W. Cowan, 1838. xi, 294 p.

Copy belonging to Alexandre C. Lindsay, 1845.

29
JEAN ANTOINE BOUTHILLIER, 1782-1835

Traité d'arithmétique pour l'usage des écoles.

Québec: J. Neilson, 1809. [6], 144 p.

Bouthillier was surveyor and editor of the newspaper the *Canadien* in 1807 and 1808. His *Traité d'arithmétique* was the first manual of this type in Lower Canada and was reprinted many times. Copy belonging to Paul Côté (1785-1855) who moved to Bic in 1818, and is the ancestor of an important family in the history of Bic. This copy contains the bookplate of his grandson, Louis-Napoléon, militia captain and one of the mayors of Bic.

30
REV. JAMES WADDELL, ED.

Willcolkes's and Fryer's New and Much Admired System of Arithmetic and Mental Calculations...

Prince Edward Island: Printed and published by J.D. Haszard, 1837. x, 144 p.

27 A Catechism of the History of Newfoundland.

29 Traité d'arithmétique pour l'usage des écoles.

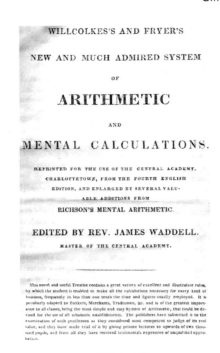

30 Willcolkes's and Fryer's New and Much Admired System of Arithmetic and Mental Calculations...

This work was printed to be used at Charlottetown's Central Academy where Rev. Waddell was master.

31

C.F. LHOMOND, 1727-1794

Élémens de la grammaire latine, à l'usage des collèges.
Nouvelle édition.

Québec: J. Neilson, 1813. 228 p.

Copy belonging to John Daly in 1832. Another example of an Anglophone student using a French-language schoolbook.

32

JENNET ROY

History of Canada for the Use of Schools and Families.

Montreal: H. Ramsay, 1854. viii, 282, [2] p.

33

JENNET ROY

Histoire du Canada à l'usage des écoles et des familles.

Montréal: H. Ramsay, 1854. vi, 293 p.

Roy's work was published in English and translated into French the same year. One can see from these examples that the readers could use editions published in their second language. In 1857, O. Durocher of Longueuil

used this book to learn English by writing in certain difficult words in French. The French language edition was owned by Dudley Baxter.

34

Fourth Book of Lessons for the Use of Schools.
New edition, revised and corrected. Published by the Direction of the Commissioners of National Education in Ireland.

Baltimore: J.B. Thompson & Co.; Halifax, N.S.: A. & W. Mackinlay, 1857. 312 p.

Reprints of the Irish National Series of Schoolbooks in stereotype.

35

JOHN HERBERT SANGSTER, 1831-1904

Elementary Arithmetic, in Decimal Currency: Designed for the Use of Canadian Schools. Third edition.

Montreal: J. Lovell; Toronto: R. & A. Miller, 1862. 224 p.

An example of the Lovell's Series of School Books.

36

Reading-Book. No. IV. Illustrated.

Halifax: A. & W. Mackinlay & Co., [circa 1865]. 190 p.

An example of the Nova Scotia School Series.

36 Reading-Book.

37

JOHN ALEXANDER BOYD, 1837-1916

A Summary of Canadian History: From the Time of Cartier's Discovery to the Present Day.

Toronto: J. Campbell, 1868. 124 p.

Example of Campbell's British American Series of School Books.

38

JAMES SMITH, 1821-1888

Les Éléments de l'agriculture à l'usage de la jeunesse.

Québec: Atelier typographique du "Canadien", 1862. 118 p.

The author was professor of agriculture at the agricultural industrial college in Rimouski. Copy containing the circular letter distributed with the work.

39

[JEAN-MARIE RAPHAEL LE JEUNE, 1855-1930]

Chinook and Shorthand Rudiments, with which the Chinook Jargon and the Wawa Shorthand Can Be Mastered without a Teacher in a Few Hours.

By the editor of the "Kamloops Wawa." Kamloops, B.C., 1898. 14 p.

Oblate Father Le Jeune was the editor of the Kamloops Wawa in which he printed Chinook jargon in roman orthography and in an adaptation of the Duployé shorthand. Chinook jargon was used extensively in contacts between the Natives and the settlers of British Columbia.

40

Guide des jeunes amoureux pour parler et écrire.

Québec: Imprimerie de L.P. Normand, 1863. 32 p.

Certain manuals, inspired by European works, were designed to supply model letters for all occasions, even that of love.

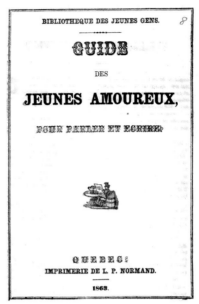

40   *Guide des jeunes amoureux pour parler et écrire.*

39   *Chinook and Shorthand Rudiments...*

Immigration and Transportation

Up until 1815, most of the immigrants to Canada were Americans, mainly Loyalists. After 1815, emigration from the British Isles increased due to a number of factors: changes in agricultural land use affecting tenants, overpopulation, failure of the potato crops, introduction of machines in the textile and other industries, and, of course, post-war economic depression. The British government encouraged this migration in order to strengthen British presence in North America and counterbalance the American influence in Canada. Between 1829 and 1836, there was an increase in emigration to Canada, especially Upper Canada, mainly due to the movement of the poverty-stricken Irish, lower passage fees, and government financial incentives. The Canadian rebellions of 1837 caused a temporary decrease in immigration which picked up again after 1842. Not all immigrants stayed, many used the cheaper passage and more lenient bureaucracy to come to Canada before continuing on to the United States.

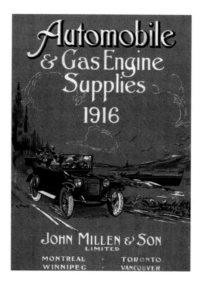

A great number of emigration manuals and settlers' guides were published for colonists intending to make their way to Canada. Initially designed to properly inform them of pitfalls and difficulties they might encounter in their voyage, these manuals tended to be somewhat biased in their description of the specific settlements they were advocating. Along with giving advice on choosing the appropriate ship, preparing for the sea voyage, customs and currency regulations, and the routes to follow to reach the intended settlement, these manuals attempted to define the ideal immigrant: hardworking, honest and of good moral character. Many guides contained letters of praise for their adopted land written by immigrants – some were known to receive a stipend – designed to convince the undecided.

As the century progressed, emigrant guides evolved, and concentrated more on descriptions of the homestead than the passage over, emphasizing free land and good opportunities.

After Confederation, and especially in the 1880s, even government pamphlets encouraging immigrants to settle in Western Canada could not convince them – and even established Canadians at that – not to move to the booming economic centres of the United States.

The tide turned when Clifford Sifton was named Minister of the Interior in charge of immigration, a position he occupied from 1896 to 1905. Under his influence, immigration literature was published in many languages and distributed throughout Western Europe and Scandinavia. The resultant increase in migration coincided with an important, if not always permanent, movement towards the Klondyke goldfields.

Transportation is included with immigration since they both concern movement from one country, one province or one village to another. The ships which carried immigrants to Canada, as well as the schooners – and later the steamships – which navigated the Saint Lawrence River and the Atlantic coast, depended heavily on sailing directions. During the 1820s and beyond, Canada began developing its own transportation infrastructure. Canals were built and railway lines were constructed. This development in transportation coincided with growing industrialization, technological advances, and changes in the economy – due in part to the termination of the Navigation Laws and the British Corn Laws as well as the signing of the Reciprocity Treaty in 1854. The economy was slowly moving from a colonial one, with England as the main partner, to a continental one emphasizing trade within the different parts of British North America and the United States. Over the course of this transition, the railroad had become the most common and economical means of transporting people and goods, including books, newspapers, and the mail.

Some of the information required to use the new means of transportation, which eventually included the automobile and the airplane, are shown in these exhibition cases. As travel for business and pleasure increased, city and regional guidebooks appeared, containing an expanded version of the information previously found in emigrant guides.

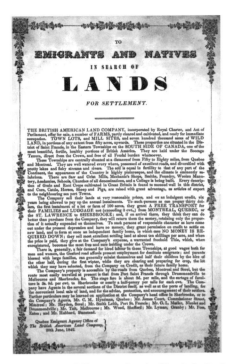

44 To Emigrants and Natives in Search of Lands for Settlement.

41

In His Majesty's Province of Upper Canada. Forty Thousand Acres of Land to Be Granted for Ever, in the Township of Norwich, ...a Most Healthy Situation on the Banks of Lake Ontario...Cork, 1st November, 1794.

Cork [Ireland], 1794.

A very early Irish advertisement designed to lure settlers to Upper Canada. It states that "All religions are tolerated...no taxes or thytes are paid...and tradesmen of all denominations are in great request." It was rather unusual to advertise for tradesmen rather than farmers.

42

PETER RUSSELL, 1733-1808. [UPPER CANADA ADMINISTRATOR FROM 1796 TO 1799]

Proclamation: Peter Russell, Esq., President, Administering the Government of Upper-Canada...Fifteenth Day of December...One Thousand Seven Hundred and Ninety-Eight.

York [Upper Canada]: Printed by William Waters and Titus G. Simons, [1798].

Broadside concerning grants of 200 acres of land to United Empire Loyalists and the exemption of payment of fees.

43

UPPER CANADA. EXECUTIVE COUNCIL

Whereas the Persons Whose Names are Hereunder Specified, Did, Through Their Agent Simon Zelotes Watson, Receive the Promise of Government for a Single Location of Two Hundred Acres Each in the Township of Westminster...York, 8th February, 1812.

[Toronto, 1812].

Many settlers, such as those listed in this broadside, did not arrive in time to take possession of their reserved lots, and consequently the land was then open to general application and settlement.

44

BRITISH AMERICAN LAND COMPANY. QUEBEC EMIGRANT AGENCY OFFICE

To Emigrants and Natives in Search of Lands for Settlement.

[Quebec (Province)?, 1842?].

An offer of land in the district of St. Francis, in the Eastern Townships of Quebec, listing conditions of sale, means of transportation, etc. Conscious of the financial plight of many immigrants, it does not hesitate to recommend: "...parents blessed with large families, can generally subsist themselves and half their children by the hire of the other half, during the first winter."

45

JOHN LEWELLIN, 1778-1879

Emigration. Prince Edward Island: A Brief But Faithful Account of This Fine Colony; Shewing Some of Its Advantages as a Place of Settlement; Addressed to Those British Farmers, and Others, Who Are Determined to Emigrate, and Try Their Fortune in a New Country.

Charlotte-Town: Printed and published by James D. Haszard Royal Gazette Office, 1832. vi, 28, [1] p.

First published in London in 1826, this manual had a number of editions. Having emigrated to Prince Edward Island in 1824, the author recommends the island for the fertility of the soil, the quality of the fishing, and as an ideal location for commerce. According to the author, an advantage of this location was that emigrants would not have to transport their goods as far as they would if they settled in Lower or Upper Canada. For the sea voyage, the author suggests:

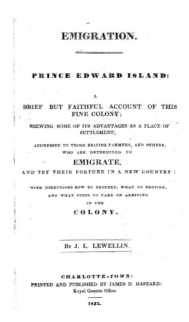

EMIGRATION.

PRINCE EDWARD ISLAND:

A

BRIEF BUT FAITHFUL ACCOUNT OF THIS
FINE COLONY;

SHEWING SOME OF ITS ADVANTAGES AS A PLACE OF
SETTLEMENT,

ADDRESSED TO THOSE BRITISH FARMERS, AND OTHERS,
WHO ARE DETERMINED TO

EMIGRATE,

AND TRY THEIR FORTUNE IN A NEW COUNTRY :

WITH DIRECTIONS HOW TO PROCEED, WHAT TO PROVIDE,
AND WHAT STEPS TO TAKE ON ARRIVING
IN THE

COLONY.

By J. L. LEWELLIN.

CHARLOTTE-TOWN:
PRINTED AND PUBLISHED BY JAMES D. HASZARD:
Royal Gazette Office.

1832.

45 *Emigration. Prince Edward Island*

"Don't forget to put up your Bible, with any other good books, and school books for your children, if you have a family." A list of 22 subscribers, purchasing a total of 300 copies, is printed at the end of the book.

46

A Few Plain Directions for Persons Intending to Proceed as Settlers to His Majesty's Province of Upper Canada, in North America: ... by an English Farmer Settled in Upper Canada.

London: Printed for Baldwin, Cradock, and Joy..., 1820. vii, 100 p.

In his preface, the author writes: "I have no hesitation in saying that the British Colonies, particularly the province of Upper Canada, are more suitable for British emigrants, whether agriculturalists or mechanics, than the United States, and that they would there have better prospects of success, as well as the enjoyment of a greater degree of happiness and contentment" (p. 3).

47

MARTIN DOYLE

Hints on Emigration to Upper Canada: Especially Addressed to the Middle and Lower Classes in Great Britain and Ireland. 2nd ed. enl.

Dublin: W. Curry, June, 1832. vi, 92 p.

Five thousand copies were printed of each of the three editions of this popular guide, designed especially for the Irish emigrant. The author states: "I do not want to strip the country of its population – the landlords of their tenantry – or the smug farmer of his comfortable subsistence, by urging any wild and doubtful speculation...but I am very desirous to rescue from overwhelming distress, those who struggle without succeeding, paupers in

everything but in health and strength, and able bodies, and willing minds" (p. 2). He favours Upper Canada over Lower Canada which, according to the author, has harsher winters, and the Maritime provinces which are covered by fog much of the year! The work ends with letters from settlers, a characteristic of many emigrant guides.

48

ALEXANDER CARLISLE BUCHANAN, SR.

Official Information for Emigrants, Arriving at New York, and Who Are Desirous of Settling in the Canadas.

Montreal: Printed at the Gazette Office, 1834. 12 p.

This free publication gave information to the settler arriving in New York or Quebec City, on changing his currency, and on transportation to Upper and Lower Canada. Buchanan was the first chief emigration agent in Quebec. Before his retirement, brought about by repeated exposure to diseases, Buchanan had provided landing money, food, clothes, and advice to thousands of immigrants.

49

JOHN LAMBLY

Sailing Directions for the River St. Lawrence, from Cape Chatt to the Island of Bic...

Quebec: New Printing Office, 1808. 28 p.

An experienced mariner, Lambly later became harbour master in Quebec City. These are probably the first sailing directions for the St. Lawrence printed in Canada. They were designed for local seamen.

THE Author of these Sailing Directions thinks proper to mention that in the year 1797, he first came to Quebec and particularly felt the want of some Sailing Directions to Navigate the river St. Lawrence. The repeated opinions of Seamen and fellow Captains since that time have fully confirmed his first opinion that a book of this kind would be of great use, and he having been employed three years as Commander of the Government Vessel stationed off Father Point ; he has had an opportunity of making the following Remarks. They are thrown together just as they occurred to him while on the spot; and as the Book is designed to come into the hands of seamen only, he flatters himself that the language will be easily understood.

This book is designed to accompany a general chart of the river from Cape Chatt to Bic Island ; and four particular ones, one of the Island of Bic, with the passage, and anchorage to the Southward of it ; one of Saint Nicolas Harbour, one of Trinity Bay, and one of Manicougan great Shoal and Bay, on a larger scale than General Chart.

But as the plates cannot be engraved at Quebec, the Charts must be sent to England, for them, and he hopes that they will accompany the book next year.

The latitudes and longitudes of the principal places in this river has never been accurately ascertained I believe, but taking the situation of Saint Nicholas Harbour for a true departure (from Hamilton Moore or Mallham), the bearings and distances are worked from them, as circumstances allowed. But seamen will all agree with me that lat. and long. are not very essential in navigating this river to the Westward from Cape Chatt.

THE AUTHOR.

Quebec, January, 1808. *Lambly*

49 *Sailing Directions for the River St. Lawrence, from Cape Chatt to the Island of Bic...*

50

HENRY WOLSEY BAYFIELD, 1795-1885

Directions de navigation pour l'Ile de Terreneuve et la côte du Labrador et pour le golfe et le fleuve St-Laurent...

traduit de l'anglais par Thomas T. Nesbitt.

Québec: Elzéar Vincent, 1864. 203 p.

With the proliferation of shipping and the increased presence of steamers, it was imperative to review the charts which had been drawn by J.F.W. DesBarres during the 18th century, especially for the River and Gulf of St. Lawrence. Bayfield's work was used for many years. English editions of Bayfield's work were published in London but it was important to have French translations.

This is the French translation of *Sailing Directions for the Island of Newfoundland and the Adjacent Coast of Labrador...*(London, 1855).

51

An Almanack for the Year of Our Lord, 1811, ...

by Theophrastus.

Halifax: Printed and sold by John Howe & Son, [1810].

Many of the early Halifax almanacs were used by people connected with the sea. This copy was owned by the captain of a schooner who filled the blank pages with the detailed description of weather conditions, the direction and force of the winds, and even the log of a trip from Halifax to Quebec City. The almanac was a professional journal, but could also be a very personal one, as the captain wrote:

"Wednesday morning the 7th August at 1/2 past one George Henry born" and, but a few months later, "Friday morning 8th Nov. at 6 o'clock George Henry died aged 3 months & one day – & buried on Sunday the 10th following at the place of internment in St. John's suburbs, Quebec."

52

CANADIAN PACIFIC RAILWAY

What Women Say of the Canadian North-West. A Simple Statement of the Experiences of Women Settled in All Parts of Manitoba and the North-West Territories.

[London: H. Blacklock & Co., 1886]. 48 p.

In its negotiations with the government, the Canadian Pacific Railway had received 25 million acres of land, and had made some of it available for sale to settlers. This pamphlet, issued out of the CPR's London office, attempted to convince settlers to come to Western Canada by reprinting letters from women who had emigrated. These efforts attracted only a very few immigrants during that period.

53

CANADA. DEPARTMENT OF THE INTERIOR

Where and How ... [text in English]
Wo und wie, ...[text in German]

53   Hvarest och huru [text in Swedish].

Hvor og hvorledes [text in Norwegian]
Hvarest och huru [text in Swedish]

Ottawa, 1903. 22 page folder with large map on reverse.

The period between 1896 and 1905, which saw Clifford Sifton as minister of the interior in charge of immigration, was the most active and successful in promoting Western immigration and in publishing immigration literature in many languages.

54*

CANADA. DEPARTMENT OF THE INTERIOR AND DEPARTMENT OF NATIONAL REVENUE

How to Enter Canada...

Ottawa, 1928. 4 p.

The growing use of the automobile and the increase in leisure travel of the 1920s saw a need for rules and regulations concerning frequent visitors from the United States.

55

How to Get to the Klondyke: The Safest, Best and Cheapest Route to Yukon Gold Fields is via the Regina, Prince Albert, Green Lake and Fort McMurray.

Prince Albert, Sask., 1898. 29 p.

The find of placer gold in a tributary of the Klondike River in August 1896 set off a stampede of prospectors and adventurers from all over Canada and the United States. For the next few years, hundreds of guides were printed, even in Europe, for persons willing to travel to that region. The contents are very reminiscent of the "emigrant guides" shown in this exhibition. Steamboat and railway companies, taking

* This item is not included in the exhibition.

55 How to Get to the Klondyke.

59 From Niagara to the Sea! (See colour insert p. iii).

advantage of this new market, printed many of these guides and brochures designed to get the prospectors to their destination.

56

The Great Gold Belt of the Yukon, Reached by Rail, Ocean and River.

[Ontario?: Canadian Pacific Railway Co., 1897]. 6 p.

57

DOMINICK DALY, 1798-1868

Schedule of Tolls, to be Paid for Passing through the St. Ann's Lock: Boats or Barges, with Whatever Cargoes Laden, Except Salt and Sea Coal.

[Quebec?, 184-?].

Rates for steam boats and barges with their cargo of timber going through the locks at Ste. Anne de Bellevue, at the junction of the St. Lawrence and Ottawa rivers.

58

LOWER CANADA. COURT OF GENERAL QUARTER SESSIONS OF THE PEACE (DISTRICT OF MONTREAL)

Rules and Regulations for Ferries / Règles et règlemens des traversiers.

[Montreal, between 1830 and 1845].

Rates for the ferry connecting Chambly to St. Mathias. Following the ferry regulations, each operator had to write in manuscript the different rates for calèches, horses, oxen, cows, foot passengers, calves or sheep.

59

RICHELIEU & ONTARIO NAVIGATION CO.

From Niagara to the Sea!

Montreal, 1901 (printed in Buffalo, N.Y.).

Trip from Toronto to Chicoutimi by steamer.

60

NORTH SHORE NAVIGATION COMPANY OF ONTARIO LTD.

Pocket Time Table. Royal Mail Line.

Collingwood, Ont., 1894.

61*

THE NORTH AMERICAN TRANSPORTATION CO. LTD.

Time-Table between Dalhousie, N.B. and Gaspé, Qué.

Steamer *Admiral*. Bi-weekly. [S.l.], 1900.

62

GRAND TRUNK RAILWAY COMPANY OF CANADA

Grand Trunk Railway of Canada Passenger Time Tables: June 9, 1861.

[Montreal: H. Rose, 1861].

Incorporated in 1852, the Grand Trunk Railway was designed to link the port of Halifax to the rest of Canada. This timetable for the lines connecting Montreal-Toronto-Detroit, Montreal-Portland and Montreal-Levis dates from the beginning and still modest years of the company. By Confederation, the Grand Trunk Railway was the largest railway system in the world.

* This item is not included in the exhibition.

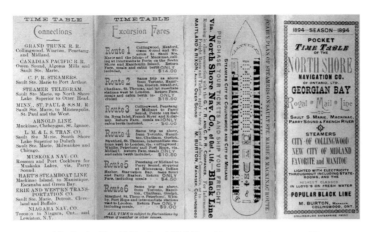

60   *Pocket Time Table. Royal Mail Line. (See colour insert p. ii).*

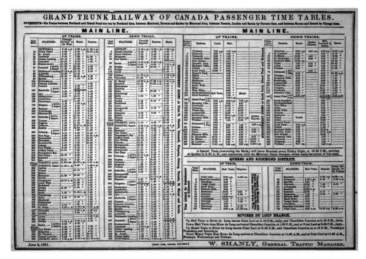

62   *Grand Trunk Railway of Canada Passenger Time Tables: June 9, 1861.*

63

QUEBEC AND LAKE ST. JOHN RAILWAY

Chemin de fer de Quebec et du Lac St. Jean: a partir de lundi, 9 janvier 1888, les trains circuleront comme suit, excepté le dimanche.

[Quebec: Quebec and Lake St. John Railway, 1887].

Rates for passengers and agricultural products on the railway line between Quebec and Chicoutimi.

64

CANADIAN NATIONAL RAILWAYS

Billets à prix réduits...

[Toronto: Canadian National Railways, circa 1949]. 1 p.

Contains fares and timetable for the Valleyfield-Toronto-Detroit-Chicago line.

65

VANCOUVER ISLAND COACH LINES LTD.

Bus Time Tables 1944.

Victoria, B.C.: Clarke Printing Co. Ltd., May 1, 1944.

66

HAMILTON BUS LINES LTD.

Time Table No. 2. Effective May 10, [n.d.].

From Hamilton to St. Catharines.

67

JOHN MILLEN & SON LTD.

Catalogue No. 55.

Montreal: J. Millen, 1916. 219, v p.

Early catalogue of automobile and gas engine supplies.

68

TRANS-CANADA AIR LINES

Schedules, Dec. 1, 1940.

Trans-Canada Airlines (TCA) was founded in April 1937, and the first passenger service shown here from Moncton, N.B. to Vancouver was inaugurated on February 15, 1940.

66   *Time Table No. 2.*

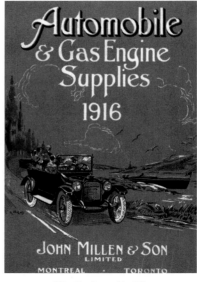

67   *Catalogue No. 55.*

69   The Picture of Quebec.

69
GEORGE BOURNE, 1780-1845 AND D. AND JAMES SMILLIE (1807-1885)
The Picture of Quebec.

Quebec: D. and J. Smillie, 1829. 139 p.

One of the first tourist guides published in Quebec. The engravings were done by James Smillie.

70*

The Hand-Book of Quebec: A Compendium of Information for the Use of Strangers Visiting the City and Its Environs Handbook of Quebec.

Quebec: Printed by T. Cary, 1850. 18, [2] p.

71

The Quebec Guide: Being a Concise Account of All the Places of Interest in and about the City and Country Adjacent, together with a Carters' Tariff, and Table of Railroad Distances throughout the Province.

Quebec: Sinclair, 1857. 48 p.

72
GEORGE H. HACKSTAFF
New Guide Book of Niagara Falls for Strangers.

Niagara Falls, Ont.: Printed at the Iris Office, 1850. 31, [17] p.

Most of the guides to Niagara Falls, and there were hundreds, were printed in Great Britain or the United States, quite often in Buffalo and Albany, and were illustrated using techniques not readily available in Canada. This modest Canadian guide gives a brief description of what to see, and includes many advertisements which, no doubt, helped pay the printing costs.

73

The Donegana Hotel, Bill of Fare: Montréal, Sunday, August 29, 1858.

Montréal: J. Potts, Herald Office, 1858.

A prestigious hotel advertises its menu and wine list, as well as the current play at the Theatre Royal, where the Denin sisters played both Romeo and Juliet!

74
NEW BRUNSWICK. POST OFFICE
Notice to the Public, and Instructions to All Postmasters and Way-Office Keepers: ...the Following Changes Will Be Made in the Rates of Postage on Letters and Parliamentary Proceedings Passing between New-Brunswick and the United Kingdom... J. Howe P.M.G....St. John, 24th July 1854.

[Fredericton?, N.B., 1854].

In August 1854, shortly after the beginning of the Crimean War, a letter could be sent from New Brunswick to Great Britain in a number of ways: by Cunard steamer through Halifax; by the relatively new Canadian packet service from Quebec City in summer or Portland, Maine, in winter; in "closed mails" through the United States; or by United States packets. The following announcement sets the different rates, all having been lowered except for the United States packet service.

73   The Donegana Hotel, Bill of Fare: Montréal, Sunday, August 29, 1858.

* This item is not included in the exhibition.

Household and Family

It was in the home that most books were used, and the most common was certainly the almanac, often hung by a string somewhere in the kitchen. Hundreds of different types of almanacs were published in Canada, and some will be seen throughout the different sections of this exhibition. Although religious, agricultural, medical or simply general information made up the majority of the text, it was the calendar pages that were the most used. Interleaved with blank pages – and later lined pages – for notes, these almanacs became daily journals. Nineteenth-century Canadians did not use the almanac to plan ahead, as the agenda is used today, but wrote what they did and when: almanacs recorded family histories, planting of crops, social events, letters sent, sales made and, of course, the weather. For those who used only the calendar pages, sheet almanacs or broadside calendars were published, showing all the information for the year on one sheet. They were the ancestors of our wall calendars.

When lists of householders were needed, for security, electoral, or business reasons, city directories appeared – an early form of our telephone directory. These directories became yearly publications only in mid-century when advertisements by retailers paid for the cost of printing.

At the end of the 19th century, retailers such as T. Eaton & Co., printed catalogues to be distributed across the land, and it is often said that no family was without one.

Cooking skills were rarely learned from books, but passed on from mother to daughter along with family recipes. Nevertheless, many almanacs contained recipes, and imported cookbooks became more and more popular as the food industry progressed. Some food companies produced their own cookbooks, using them as a form of advertising.

The ancestor of our modern wall calendar was the sheet almanac or calendar. It contained much of the information found in almanacs and showed all twelve months at a glance. The evolution of the use of the calendar, from a record of past events, to an agenda, had begun. As the *New Dominion Calendar for 1869* points out: "This calendar should be neatly mounted, by pasting on a board or canvas and hung where it may remain throughout the year."

75

The Montreal Calendar for 1840...

Montreal: J. Lovell, [1839].

This calendar contains, on one sheet, much of the information also found in almanacs, including facts regarding the military, the courts of justice, the post office rates, etc. It was distributed to numerous sales outlets in the city.

76

Calendrier de Québec pour l'année 1854...

[Quebec]: Publié et à vendre chez Robert Middleton, [1853].

This calendar contains mainly information on the clergy.

77

The New Dominion Calendar for 1869.

Montreal: J. Dougall & Son, [1868].

An early illustrated calendar apparently printed as a supplement to the *Canadian Messenger*, the *Montreal Weekly Witness*, the *Montreal Witness*, the *Dominion Monthly*, and the *Daily Witness*.

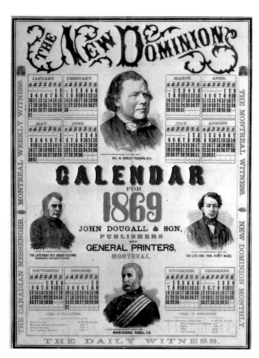

77 The New Dominion Calendar for 1869.

78

JACQUES JUDAH LYONS, 1813-1877 AND ABRAHAM DE SOLA, 1825-1882

A Jewish Calendar for Fifty Years...together with an Introductory Essay on the Jewish Calendar System.

Montreal: John Lovell, 1854.

The first book of wholly Jewish content to be printed in Canada contains a table, with two Hebrew columns, listing the appropriate Torah readings for the year's Sabbaths.

79*

Indian Calendar for 1907.

[Kamloops, B.C.?: Missionary Press?, 1906].

J-M.R. Le Jeune (1855-1930) was the editor of the newspaper *Kamloops Wawa* in Chinook jargon. This calendar was probably intended for subscribers. On the reverse, Father Le Jeune has written his grocery list.

80

Der hochdeutsche neu-schottländische Calender, auf das Jahr, nach der heilbringenden Geburt unsers Herrn Jesu Christi, 1788. [The High German Nova Scotian Calendar for the Year 1788.]

Halifax: Anthon Henrich, 1787. [44] p.

This is Anthony Henry's first almanac printed in German and is the earliest German-language publication in Canada. The German population of the Halifax area usually imported almanacs and other publications in their language from Pennsylvania. Henry seems to have continued printing these until at least 1796. The woodcuts appear to have been made locally. This copy belonged to Georg Philipp Brehm of Halifax (with his signature dated 1788).

81

The Quebec Almanac; and British American Royal Kalendar, for the Year 1819.

Quebec: J. Neilson, [1818]. 235 p.

The Quebec Almanac was one of the more useful almanacs and contained many characteristics of a

78 A Jewish Calendar for Fifty Years.

80 Der hochdeutsche neu-schottländische Calender.

* This item not included in the exhibition.

directory: names of members of the military, and of religious, political and judiciary bodies. The owner of this copy, Militia Captain Oliver Barker, updated much of the information over the year and even had some harsh comments and important corrections concerning the geographical information provided (p. 190-191). On the blank endleaves, he writes: "A City Directory would be a very great accommodation to the Public, & to Strangers, & would amply remunerate the compiler I think." Someone in Montreal may have heard him since the first directory for that city was published the same year (1819). From the Victor Morin and Georges-Alphonse Daviault collections.

82

The York Almanac, and Provincial Calendar, for the Year 1821...

York [Ont.]: Printed and sold at the Upper-Canada Gazette office, [1821]. 53 p.

This first *York Almanac* was used by someone in the legal profession, possibly a member of the Anderson family. It contains a few professional entries, corrections to names of office holders, but also manuscript notes pertaining to the planting of vegetables, results of fishing trips, letters sent abroad, and on April 6 this short but enthusiastic entry: "Saw a butterfly." It is interesting to note that these entries, dated 1824, were made in an almanac for 1821.

83

The New-Brunswick Almanack, for the Year of Our Lord 1847...

Saint John: Printed by Henry Chubb & Company and sold at the Courier Office, [1846].

This almanac shows the January calendar with its accompanying blank page containing detailed information on the temperature for each day, even at different times of the day, and the amount of snow fall.

84*

Dominion Almanac for 1875. Being a Supplement to "Montreal Weekly Witness."

[Montreal: Witness Job Office, 1874].

Mainly used to advertise its newspapers and a few services, this type of almanac included recipes, humorous stories, and calendars containing famous quotes, mixed with facts and figures about the *Witness*. A rather aggressive form of advertising.

85*

Annual Edition. Hebrew Almanac for the Year 5686 (1925-1926). From Sept. 19, 1925 to Sept. 8, 1926

[followed by Hebrew title].

New York: Hebrew Publishing Company, 1925.

Hebrew almanac printed in the United States but distrib-

uted in Montreal by L. Holstein & Co. Ltd., steamship passenger agents. This company had advertising wrappers printed in English and Hebrew.

86

THOMAS DOIGE

An Alphabetical List of the Merchants, Traders, and Housekeepers, Residing in Montreal...

Montreal: James Lane, 1819. 192 p.

This is the earliest Montreal directory. It contains numbers for each dwelling, some of which had not previously been assigned. In his preface, the compiler encourages householders to place these numbers on their houses. Copy belonging to P. Lussier.

87*

ROBERT WALTER STUART MACKAY, CIRCA 1809-1854

The Montreal Directory for 1844-5...

Montreal: Printed and sold by Lovell and Gibson, [1844]. 300 p.

The Mackay directories evolved into the famous Lovell directories after the author's death.

88

THOMAS HENRI GLEASON

The Quebec Directory for 1822...

Quebec: Neilson and Cowan, 1822. xi, 142 p.

The first 19th-century Quebec City directory (after Hugh Mackay's directories of 1790 and 1791). Aside from a listing of merchants, traders and householders, it contains a description of public and commercial services, the Rules and Regulations of Police, and some advertisements. A very useful large plan of the city was engraved on copper and sold with the book. In his preface, the compiler addresses the issue of the numbering of houses: "In particularizing the numbers of the houses, no regard has been paid to those already placed upon them unless found correct. The majority of them are incorrect, but the numbers inserted in the Directory will be found accurate when a general numbering takes place."

89

GEORGE WALTON

The City of Toronto and the Home District Commercial Directory and Register, with Almanack and Calendar for 1837...

Toronto: Printed by T. Dalton and W.J. Coates, [1836]. 48, 192, 45 p.

This is the second Toronto directory (the first was for 1833-34). The compiler was a notary. It is divided into three parts: the almanac; the list of inhabitants, and their occupation, of the city of Toronto, and of the counties of York and Simcoe; and a listing of commercial and public institutions not contained in the almanac section. This copy belonged to eminent Toronto lawyer and jurist John Godfrey Spragge (1806-1884).

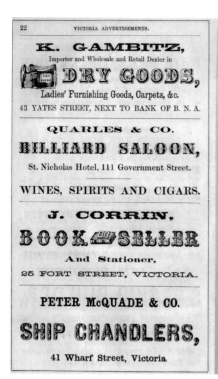

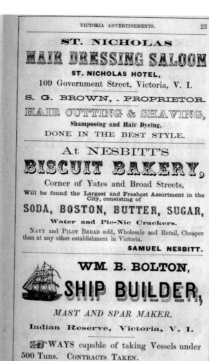

90 *The British Columbian and Victoria Guide and Directory...*

91 *Winnipeg Directory and Manitoba Almanac...*

90

FREDERICK P. HOWARD AND GEORGE BARNETT, COMPILERS

The British Columbian and Victoria Guide and Directory for 1863...

Victoria, V.I. [Vancouver Island]: Office of the British Columbian and Victoria Directory, 1863. 216 p.

The first directory published in British Columbia. Although printing had already been established in the colony, it was printed in San Francisco by Towne & Bacon. It contains a list of residents of Victoria and New Westminster and is especially valuable for the advertisements. It took another 15 years for the next directory to appear.

91

Winnipeg Directory and Manitoba Almanac for 1876. Postal Guide and Handbook of General Infromation [*sic*].

Winnipeg: Cook & Fletcher, [1875].

This early Manitoba directory combined information from the traditional almanac, including many advertisements, postal information, and a 15-page listing of the "Male adult residents of Winnipeg."

92

THE T. EATON CO. LIMITED

Spring-Summer 1906 Catalogue No. 74.

Toronto, [1906]. 210 p.

93

THE T. EATON CO. LIMITED

Spring and Summer 1926.

Moncton, [1926]. 414 p.

Timothy Eaton (1834-1907) opened his first Toronto store in 1869, and published his first catalogue in 1884. Over the years, the company opened outlets throughout the country, each having its own catalogue such as this one from Moncton for 1926. An Eaton's catalogue was found in most households across Canada.

94

THE ROBERT SIMPSON COMPANY LIMITED

White Goods Catalogue No. 96. January 1906.

Toronto, [1905]. 48 p.

This company was founded by Robert Simpson (1834-1897) in 1872 in Toronto. It issued catalogues beginning in 1894. It was always a great competitor of Eaton's.

95

NERLICH & COMPANY

Catalogue No. 87: Season 1939-1940.

Toronto: The Company, 1939. 224 p.

Nerlich was founded in 1858 and specialized in china, glass, fancy goods, toys and dolls. If one judges by the price of toys, this catalogue was obviously geared to quite wealthy customers.

94 *White Goods Catalogue No. 96. January 1906.*

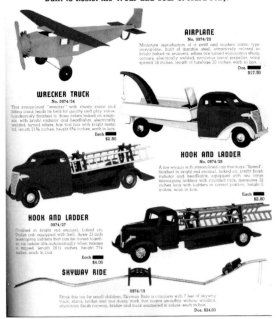

95 *Catalogue No. 87: Season 1939-1940.*
(See colour insert p. ii).

96

P.T. LÉGARÉ LIMITÉE

Catalogue No. 44.

[Ottawa?]: printed by the Mortimer Co. Ltd., [1920]. 422 p.

One of the most important merchants and manufacturers in French Canada, Pierre-Théophile Légaré (1851-1926) and his enterprise specialized in carriages and farm equipment. He was also a distributor of household articles.

97

MCCLARY MANUFACTURING CO.

Illustrated Price List for 1890.

London, Ont.: R. Southam, 1890. 159 p.

This firm was most famous for its manufacturing of stoves and hot-air furnaces. The beautifully lithographed front and back covers were the work of Barclay, Clark and Co. of Toronto.

98

SINGER SEWING MACHINE COMPANY

Singer Sewing Machines.

Canada: The Company, [circa 1913]. 24 p.

97 *Illustrated Price List for 1890.*
(See colour insert p. v).

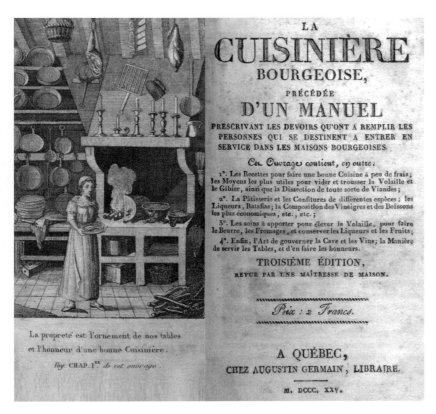

99   La Cuisinière bourgeoise...

99

MENON, 18TH CENTURY

La Cuisinière bourgeoise, précédée d'un Manuel prescrivant les devoirs qu'ont à remplir les personnes qui se destinent à entrer en service dans les maisons bourgeoises... Troisième édition revue par une maîtresse de maison.

Québec: Augustin Germain; Paris: Imprimerie J. Moronval, 1825. 312 p.

Before 1840, cookbooks used in Canada were imported, some being sold unaltered while others included a special title page printed by the Canadian bookseller. In this particular example, the complete book was printed in Paris, including the title page; the Quebec bookseller having requested a personalized title page from the French printer. This infrequent practice was designed to give a particularly local touch to a foreign work and thus attract more customers.

Menon's work is a classic in gastronomy. First printed in Paris in 1746, it went through a great many editions. As the work contains rather sophisticated recipes, requiring ingredients and produce only readily available in Europe, one wonders how useful it was to the average Canadian family.

100

Nouvelle Cuisinière canadienne: Contenant tout ce qu'il est nécessaire de savoir dans un ménage, tel que l'achat de diverses sortes de denrées, la manière de préparer les soupes grasses et maigres, cuire et assaisonner les potages et rôtis de toute espèce, [etc.]. Éd. rev., corr. et considérablement augm.

Montréal: L. Perrault, [circa 1850-1860]. 108 p.

101

Mother Hubbard's Cupboard; or, Canadian Cook Book: Over Five Hundred Practical Receipts.

Hamilton, Ont.: G.C. Briggs, 1881. 112, [16] p.

The cookbooks of the second half of the 19th century also contained practical information on washing, dying and home remedies. Some also included short poems, aphorisms or humorous stories to amuse the homemaker.

102

OGILVIE FLOUR MILLS COMPANY

Recettes Ogilvie pour la cuisinière moderne.

Montreal: Ogilvie, 1913. 123 p.

Many cookbooks were published by food companies.

103

CANADA FOOD BOARD

Potatoes and How to Cook Them.

Ottawa: Canada Food Board, 1918. 8 p.

Specialized cookbooks were published during the last two wars. They contained simple recipes using the most common types of food.

Agriculture and Trades

For a great many Canadians in rural areas, agriculture was a full-time occupation, and for the others, a way of helping to feed the family or making a little income on the side. Before the establishment of agricultural colleges in the middle of the 19th century, only a few books were published to teach children the principles of agriculture (see the section on Children's Literature and Education). Even then, most people believed that being raised on a farm was enough to make anyone a good farmer. Later in the century, and certainly during the 20th century when agriculture became a large business, publications concerning new methods or new crops became more plentiful.

As in the case of agriculture, most trades were learned on the job and not from books, and it was not uncommon for Canadians to hold two or three jobs to make ends meet. The books exhibited here include mathematical tables used by lumber merchants, accountants, and owners of small businesses. The development of manufacturing and retailing called for skills such as stenography, the ability to compute wages, profit margins and interest rates, along with the books and manuals needed to both acquire and use these capabilities. As the economy grew, broadsides advertising manufactured goods, agricultural products, and land sales became common sights in market areas and storefronts.

104

The Canadian Farmers' Almanac, for the Year of Our Lord 1836...

Sherbrooke and Stanstead, L[ower] C[anada]: Walton & Gaylord, [1835].

Unlike most almanacs, which contained only general information, this one was intended for farmers, and included a long article on the wool industry, potato farming, and of course the plea for temperance. Next to each month, were printed memorandum pages which the owner of this copy used to record the weather.

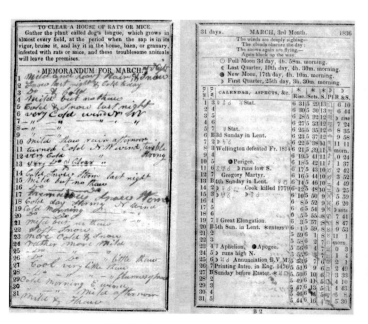

104 The Canadian Farmers' Almanac...

105 *Combined Mowing and Reaping Machines...*

105

JOHN SMITH

Combined Mowing and Reaping Machines...: Farmers, Send Your Orders Early...

[Montreal, 1857].

An advertisement from a distributor of horse-drawn farm machinery located at St. Gabriel Locks in Montreal in 1857. To enhance its ad, the company used a wood engraving by John Henry Walker (1831-1899) who had recently established his business in Montreal. Walker also provided numerous illustrations for periodicals and magazines.

106

R. & A. Miller's Canadian Farmers Almanac for the Year of Our Lord 1855.

Montreal: R. & A. Miller, [1854].

The *Miller's Canadian Farmers Almanac* was printed by John Lovell in Montreal in editions of 30 000 copies in the 1860s and of up to 60 000 copies in the 1870s. It was distributed by many bookstores and stationers in Quebec and Ontario such as John Drurie in Ottawa, and Larmonth & Macarthur in St. Andrew. These "publishers" would have wrappers and title pages specially printed with their name and advertisements, but most of the text remained the same. It was a very popular publication since many households, although not earning their living by farming, were either growing vegetables, or had farm animals.

Copy belonging to Eléazar Hays, notary public and, it seems, gentleman farmer. For the month of March, Hays has entries concerning his chickens, the first anniversary of his father's death, and the battle of Sebastopol.

107

Almanach Rolland, agricole, commercial et des familles de la Compagnie J-B. Rolland & Fils. 1913. Quarante-septième année.

[Montreal]: En vente chez tous les libraires et les principaux marchands, [1912]. 224 p.

At the time, the *Almanach Rolland* was the most popular almanac among the Francophone population of Canada. With the increase in city population, this almanac not only targeted the farmers' market, but also the whole of the French-speaking population. It even contained short stories by well-known local writers such as Rodolphe Girard – author of *Marie Calumet*. There were also adds promoting certain concepts of beauty, including one aimed "at skinny and weak men and women of Canada and the United States."

108

WILLIAM RENNIE, 1835-1910

Successful Farming: How to Farm for Profit, the Latest Methods. Revised edition.

Toronto: W. Rennie's Sons, 1915. 254 p.

A key figure in the development of agriculture, William Rennie was the founder of the company which provided agricultural and horticultural seeds to all of Canada from 1870 to 1961. In his book, Rennie described scientific methods which could improve greatly the yield of the farms. A new type of farming had begun.

109

J.M. DE COURTENAY

The Canada Vine Grower: How Every Farmer in Canada May Plant a Vineyard and Make His Own Wine.

Toronto: James Campbell & Son, 1866. 58 p.

In Canada, the first wine was made for commercial use in 1811 by Joseph Schiller on the banks of the Credit River. In 1857, Porter Adams was the first to plant vines in what is now the heart of the Niagara region. This manual is certainly one of the first on the topic.

110

G. LAROQUE

Culture et préparation du tabac. Nouveau traité.

Lévis: Mercier & Cie., 1881. 52 p.

Tobacco had been cultivated in Canada since the French Regime, but it is only during the period of this manual that it experienced an important commercial boom. Quebec was, at that time, the main producer of tobacco in the country. This was long before the appearance of the cigarette.

III Séparateurs à crème standard.
(See colour insert p. v).

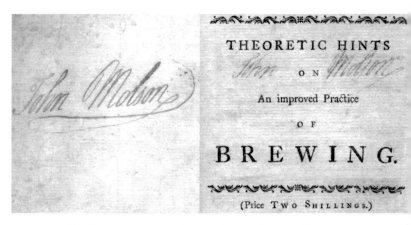

114 Theoretic Hints on an Improved Practice of Brewing Malt-Liquors.

111

THE RENFREW MACHINERY COMPANY LTD.

Séparateurs à crème standard.

Renfrew, Ont.: [Printed in Ottawa by Lowe-Martin, circa 1914].

Some companies used lithography and chromolithography to produce attractive covers for their catalogues.

112

SIR THOMAS DICK LAUDER

Directions for Taking and Curing Herrings: And for Curing Cod, Ling, Tusk, and Hake.

Saint John, N.B.: Henry Chubb & Co., 1850. 28 p.

The author was secretary to the Board of Fisheries in England. This work was reprinted in New Brunswick because it was deemed useful to local fishermen, even though most references were to the coast of Scotland.

113

Decreto per le miniere nell' Ontario...regolamento per le miniere sono stampati per informare le persone contemplate: disposizioni per la sicurezza dei minatori.

[Ontario, circa 1910].

An example of government regulations in Italian intended to be posted prominently to ensure that workers complied with safety regulations. It describes the meaning of sound signals and penalties for ignoring them. It was printed on linen to ensure durability.

114

JOHN RICHARDSON

Theoretic Hints on an Improved Practice of Brewing Malt-Liquors; Including Some Strictures on the Nature and Properties of Water, Malt, and Hops; the Doctrine of Fermentation; the Agency of Air; the Effects of Heat and Cold... The third edition, corrected.

London: Printed for G. Robinson, J. Wilkie [etc.], 1777. 74 p.

When John Molson, Sr. (1763-1836) decided, a few years after his arrival in Montreal, to open a brewery, he could not find any technical books on the subject in Canada. It was during his trip to London in 1785-1786 that he bought this book, and brought it back to Montreal. This manual was, for many years, exhibited in the reception room of the Molson Brewery in Montreal.

115

JOHN CHARLES GRANT

Tables of the Cubical Contents of Masts, Hand-Masts, Spars, and Bowsprits...

Quebec: John Neilson, 1810.

116

A Ready Reckoner for the Use of Merchants and Measurers of Timber / Comptes faits pour l'usage des commercans [sic] en bois, des mesureurs, etc. New edition corrected and enlarged. / Nouvelle édition corrigée et augmentée.

[Quebec]: John Neilson, 1816. 66 p.

117

B.H. DAY

Day's Ready Reckoner: Containing Tables for Rapid Calculations of Aggregate Values, Wages, Salary, Board, Interest Money; Timber, Plank, Board, Wood and Land Measurements...

London, Ont.: W. Bryce, 1880. 191 p.

TABLES,

SHEWING THE VALUE,

IN

HALIFAX CURRENCY,

OF

ANY SUM

OF

EXCHANGE ON LONDON,

FROM

1s. TO £1,000 STERLING,

IN A PROGRESSIVE SERIES

OF

ONE QUARTER PER CENTUM,

FROM

12½ Per Cent. Below,

TO

12½ PER CENT. ABOVE, PAR.

BY ARTHUR FESSENDEN, ACCOMPTANT,
Bank of Canada.

Montreal:
PRINTED FOR THE AUTHOR,
BY NAHUM MOWER.
1822.

118   *Tables Shewing the Value in Halifax Currency of Any Sum of Exchange on London, from 1s. to £1,000 Sterling, ...*

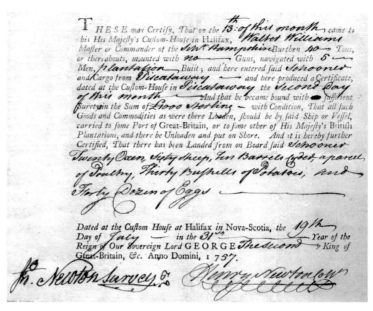

120   *These May Certify, That on the...*

These ready reckoners were indispensable to merchants and shipbuilders throughout the 19th century. Later editions included other tables for rapid calculations of interest rates, wages, land measurements, and currency.

118

ARTHUR FESSENDEN

Tables Shewing the Value in Halifax Currency of Any Sum of Exchange on London, from 1s. to £1,000 Sterling, ...

Montreal: printed for the author by Nahum Mower, 1822. 105 p.

Since the 1760s, both Halifax and New York currency had been used by merchants which resulted in much confusion since each gave the dollar a different rating. In 1821, Upper Canada made Halifax currency the only official one, as it had been in Lower Canada. With the appearance of banks in 1817, tables such as this one, converting sterling to Halifax currency became very useful.

   Copy belonging to L. Foster and S.B. Harrison, both of Toronto.

119

G. LAROCHE AND N. THIBAULT

Table des profits pour l'usage du commerce 1921/ Profits Table for Commercial Use.

Québec: N. Thibault & G. LaRoche, 1921. ix, 109 p.

120

NOVA SCOTIA. CUSTOM HOUSE (HALIFAX, N.S.)

These May Certify, That on the...

[Halifax?, N.S.: John Bushell?, between 1752 and 1757].

It is nearly certain that this customs document was printed in Halifax by John Bushell (died 1761) between 1752 and 1757. It would make it the earliest example of Canadian printing in the National Library of Canada. Unfortunately, few of these early examples of job printing have survived.

121

MATHER BYLES ALMON, 1796-1871

Prices Current.

Halifax, N.S.: J.S. Cunnabell, [circa 1829].

Prices current were some of the first imprints in Canada. This particular example is sent with a letter written by Mather Byles Almon to merchants in Madeira. It travelled by the chartered schooner *The Sophia* (named after Almon's wife). Merchants such as Almon and others in Eastern Canada used the printing press for advertisements and blanks, and for personal messages such as invitations and other forms of job printing. Almon later became one of the directors of the Bank of Nova Scotia.

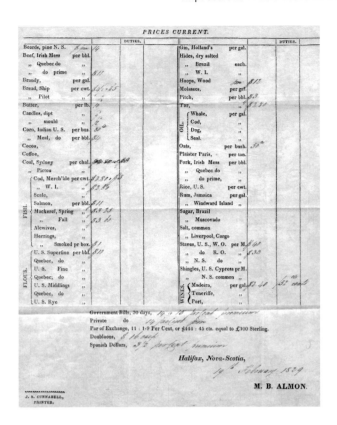

121   Prices Current.

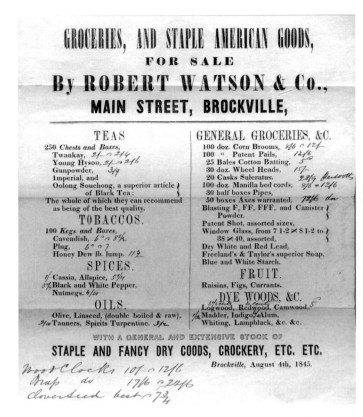

123   Groceries, and Staple American Goods, for Sale by Robert Watson
& Co., Main Street, Brockville...August 4th, 1845.

122

HALL & FAIRWEATHER

**Alexandria Flour: The Subscribers Have in Store,
Received per Recent Arrivals, 700 Barrels Alexandria
Flour, an Article to which They Would Invite the
Particular Attention of Purchasers...June 12th, 1856.**

Saint John: Avery, printer, 1856.

This advertisement argues for the quality of Alexandria flour
over New York flour, while the Brockville merchant advertises American goods.

123

ROBERT WATSON & CO.

**Groceries, and Staple American Goods, for Sale by Robert
Watson & Co., Main Street, Brockville...August 4th, 1845.**

[Brockville, Ont.: R. Watson & Co., 1845].

124

**Notice! Is Hereby Given, that W.H. Allen, Merchant,
New Hamburg, Having Made an Assignment of His
Stock, Books, Notes and Accounts to Isaac Buchanan
Esqr., Hamilton... / Zur Nachricht: Nachricht wird
hiermit ertheilt, dass William H. Allen, Kaufmann in
Neu-Hamburg...**

[New Hamburg, Ont., 1856].

Bilingual English-German broadside.

124   Notice! Is Hereby Given, that...

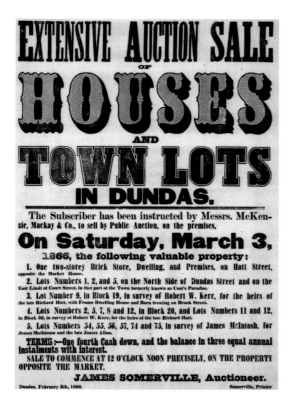

125 *Extensive Auction Sale of Houses and Town Lots in Dundas...*

126 *Great Bargains...*

125

MCKENZIE, MACKAY & CO.

Extensive Auction Sale of Houses and Town Lots in Dundas...

Dundas, Ont.: Somerville, 1866.

During the 19th century, land was often sold through public auctions.

126

WILSON AND HYMAN. WINNIPEG

Great Bargains...

[Winnipeg: Wilson and Hyman, 1871?].

Broadside advertising "recent importations," chiefly clothing, but also stationery and cigars. An importer by the name of C.H. Wilson is listed in the 1875 Winnipeg directory.

127

RÉAL ANGERS, 1812-1860

Système de sténographie, applicable au français et à l'anglais.

Québec: Imprimé pour le propriétaire par Fréchette & Cie., 1836. 16 p.

Since the first treatise on stenography printed in England during the 16th century, many systems have appeared. This work is probably the first on the subject printed in Canada and had the particularity of handling both languages.

128

W. ÉLIE

Méthode de sténographie Élie: À l'usage des écoles de la province de Québec et de ceux qui veulent écrire et relire leurs notes avec une grande facilité. Huitième édition.

Montréal, 1929. 63 p.

The increase in office work at the turn of the century created a need for stenography manuals for secretarial schools.

Judicial and Political

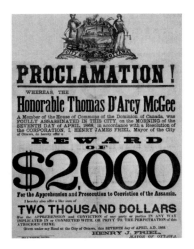

The section concerning Justice shows books used by lawyers, judges, members of elected political bodies, and officers of the militia. These works established the order of practice and provided official wording of laws. Their use was limited to a small number of well-educated men. What was crucial for most, on the other hand, was the ability to read the broadsides announcing rules and regulations which effected all Canadians.

The quest for responsible government during the 1830s and 1840s gave rise to numerous pamphlets, newspapers, and broadsides. Political propaganda issued by individuals, or later organized political parties, was always plentiful. Most early speeches could be found in the local newspapers, but some were printed in leaflet form to be distributed during rallies and public debates. As the electoral process evolved, and women gained the right to vote, the printed word became a widespread means of swaying opinion, advertising rallies, and announcing results of elections.

129

NICOLAS-GASPARD BOISSEAU, 1726-1804

Je soussigné receveur, nommé par le comité... fait à Québec, le dix huit janvier, mil sept cens soixante et cinq.

[Quebec: William Brown and Thomas Gilmore, 1765].

Most of the early printers survived by doing job printing for the government and merchants of a city. This receipt concerns the practice of billeting soldiers of the garrison in private houses. It is the earliest example of printing in the Province of Quebec held by the National Library of Canada.

130

BAS-CANADA - ADJUTANT GÉNÉRAL DES MILICES

Rules and Regulations for the Formation, Exercise & Movements of the Militia of Lower-Canada / Regles & reglemens pour la formation, l'exercice et mouvement de la milice du Bas-Canada.

Quebec: New Printing Office / Nouvelle Imprimerie, 1812. 248, [4] p.

Since the Sedentary Militia was unskilled and untrained, the publication of this manual was needed as war was approaching. War was declared on June 18, 1812.

131

LOUIS TIMOTHÉE SUZOR, 1834-1866

Aide-mémoire du carabinier volontaire: Comprenant une compilation des termes de commandement usités dans l'armée anglaise...

Québec: S. Derbishire et G. Desbarats, 1862. 52 p.

Suzor played an important role in the integration of Francophones in the militia and was an exceptional educator. His numerous manuals, for the most part translations or adaptations of English manuals, were the only

129   *Je soussigné receveur, nommé par le comité...*

131 Aide-mémoire du carabinier volontaire: Comprenant une compilation des termes de commandement usités dans l'armée anglaise...

ones available at the time and were used for generations. This handbook contains the English terms most commonly used in the French militia. Copy with the signature "Boucher de la Bruère" on the wrapper, probably Pierre-Claude Boucher de la Bruère (1808-1871), medical doctor and patriot of 1837, who was named major of the Fifth Batallion of the militia of Saint-Hyacinthe, Quebec in 1847.

132

[REGULATIONS OF POLICE FOR THE CITY OF MONTREAL]

At a Court of General Sessions of the Peace... / A une cour de sessions générales de la paix...

[Montreal, 1809].

At that time, texts of laws were read in public, that is to say "published." They were also posted in public areas. The manuscript text in the margin reads as follows: "I do hereby certify that I have on the 28th day of February, the 1st & 2d March 1809, published the within Regulations of Police in English and French Language throughout all the City of Montreal and the Suburbs, and on the 2d & 3d March, being two market days, on three different places on the old Market place only, each day. Montreal 3d March 1809. A. (?) Kollmyer, pub. cryer

I do hereby certify that I have on this 4th day of March 1809, posted up the within Regulations of Police at the Court House, on the New Market and old Market places, at the four corners of the City of Montreal, and at the French Church door. Montreal, the 4th March 1809. A. (?) Kollmyer. pub. cryer."

133 Regulations for the Governance of the Police Force...

133

WILLIAM FOSTER COFFIN, 1808-1878

Regulations for the Governance of the Police Force, Rural and City, Province of Canada: With Instructions as to the Legal Authorities and Duties of Police Constables.

Montreal: Printed by J. Starke, 1841. 39 p.

Coffin was commissioner of police for Montreal. He was instrumental in implementing a police force for the province of Quebec. On the front pastedown, one reads: "William F. Coffin, his book – made by himself. The only copy left 16 Mar. 1855."

134

J. HOWARD TOWNSEND, 1881-1927

Canadian Constables' Manual.

Toronto: Carswell, 1925. vii, 293 p.

This work was written by an inspector of the Royal Canadian Mounted Police in Saskatchewan. "Nothing has been said in this Manual regarding so-called 'Detective work'. The detection of crime is an art and not a science, therefore little can be written upon it, but much learnt by observation of all that goes on around one by those who have a natural aptitude for investigation." Times have changed!

8
......

ty's Birth Day, Pentecoste, Corpus Chrifti or Fête Dieu, St. Pierre and St. Paul, Affumption, All Saints, Conception, and Chriftmas-Day : And that on thefe feveral Holy Days, this Court fhall not fet or be held, but that on every other (Sundays excepted) it fhall fit and be held in each Term refpectively.

2. And it is ordered that the office of the Sheriff and of the Prothonotary fhall be open, and attendance therein refpectively given on every day at the hours by the Rules herein appointed, except on the above Holy-Days and Sundays. And that all the feveral rules of this Court, wherein an exception may be contained for the non.fervice or filing of pleas on a Holy-Day, fhall have relation only to the Holy-Days above declared.

SECTION II.

Of the Habits of Officers, Barrifters and Counsel.

IT is ordered, that the feveral officers of this Court, in the exercife of their refpective offices in Court, do appear habited in gowns, fuch as are worn by like officers in His Majefty's Courts in England ; and that the feveral Barrifters and Advocates do appear in Court habited in fuch gowns and bands as are worn by Barrifters of fimilar degree at Weftminfter Hall. And that this Court will not hear any matter moved by any Barrifter or Advocate, who fhall not appear fo habited when moving the fame.

135   Rules and Orders of Practice, Made for the Court of King's Bench, District of Montreal...

136   Rules and Regulations of the House of Assembly, Lower-Canada.

135
LOWER CANADA. COURT OF KING'S BENCH (DISTRICT OF MONTREAL)

Rules and Orders of Practice, Made for the Court of King's Bench, District of Montreal...

Montreal: Printed by N. Mower, 1811. 78, [18] p.

Since law books were not often reprinted and updated, lawyers would add changes to the laws in manuscript directly in the copy of the most recent edition. This copy was generously interleaved with manuscript notes by two or three previous owners, one of these being Dominique Mondelet (1799-1863), prominent lawyer and judge who signed his name on the title-page.

136
LOWER CANADA. LEGISLATURE. HOUSE OF ASSEMBLY

Rules and Regulations of the House of Assembly, Lower-Canada / Regles et reglements de la Chambre d'assemblée du Bas Canada.

Quebec: Printed for John Neilson, 1793. [4], 73, [7] p.

Copy belonging to Pierre-Paul Margane de Lavaltrie (1743-1810), French soldier at the battle of the Plains of Abraham and during the American War of Independence. Seigneur of Lavaltrie, he was a member for Warwick during the first Parliament of Lower Canada in 1792 and used this manual.

137
HUGH CHRISTOPHER THOMSON, 1791-1834

A Manual of Parliamentary Practice: With an Appendix Containing the Rules of the Legislative Council and House of Assembly of Upper Canada.

Kingston [Ont.]: H.C. Thomson, 1828. 92, [1] p.

Businessman, publisher, editor-proprietor of the *Upper Canada Herald* and member of Parliament, Hugh Christopher Thomson published the following *Manual of Parliamentary Practice* which was, in fact, a copy of Thomas Jefferson's work with the substitution of Canadian for American practices. Signature of Donald Fraser, member of Parliament, Lanark, February 13, 1833.

138
VANCOUVER ISLAND / ILE DE VANCOUVER

A Collection of the Public General Statues [i.e. Statutes] of the Colony of Vancouver Island: Passed in the Years 1859, 1860, 1861, 1862, and 1863.

Victoria, V[ancouver] I[sland]: Printed at the British Colonist Office, 1866. 1 v. (various pagings).

Some of the first examples of printing in British Columbia were acts of the colonial government of Vancouver Island. These acts, printed at different times, were bound together in one volume for the use of lawyers and office holders. This copy belonged to Coroner James Dickson in 1864, who passed it on to J. Roland Hett, notary public in 1873, clerk of the Legislative Assembly and later attorney general of the Province. It later became part of the library of Archer Evans Stringer Martin (1865-1941), lawyer and chief justice of British Columbia.

AN ACT

To Incorporate the City of Victoria.

WHEREAS, it is expedient that the District commonly known as Victoria Town should be Incorporated.

Be it enacted by the Governor, on Her Majesty's behalf, by and with the consent of the Legislative Council and Assembly of Vancouver Island and its Dependencies,

I. That from and after the passage of this Act, the tract of land specified in the first part of the first Schedule hereto, shall be incorporated as a City, to be called "the City of Victoria," the said City shall be divided into three Wards:

The Johnson street Ward, the Yates street Ward, and the James' Bay Ward.

The Johnson street Ward shall include the tract of land specified in the second part of the said first Schedule.

The Yates street Ward shall include the tract of land specified in the third part of the said first Schedule.

The James' Bay Ward, the tract of land specified in the fourth part of the said first Schedule.

II. That the government of the City

shall, subject to the provisions of this Act, be placed under the control of a Council.

The Council shall consist of a Mayor and six Councillors, possessed of the qualifications and subject to none of the disqualifications hereinafter specified, namely:

Qualifications.

III. Being a male British subject of full age.

Having resided within the Island of Vancouver and its dependencies for a space of six calendar months previous to election;

Being at and having been for three calendar months next preceding the time of election, rated on the Municipal Assessment Roll of the same City in respect of freehold to at least the value of £50, or in respect of leaseholds to at least the value of £150.

Provided always, that at the first election of a Mayor and Councillors, the qualification of such Mayor and Councillors shall, as to property, be as follows :

Possession in his own right of real property within the city to the market values,

138   A Collection of the Public General Statues [i.e. Statutes]...

139   An Act to Provide for the Safety of Her Majesty's Subjects and Others on the Highways in Upper Canada...

139

UPPER CANADA

An Act to Provide for the Safety of Her Majesty's Subjects and Others on the Highways in Upper Canada, and to Regulate the Travelling Thereon.

[Simcoe: Printed at the *Norfolk Messenger* office, circa 1853].

Broadside outlining the "rules of the road" for stage coaches, wagons, carriages and other vehicles. Today's motto against drinking and driving was also appropriate in 19th-century Canada. ..." that every person in charge of any stage coach, waggon, ...or other vehicle, horse or animal, who shall be unable to drive or ride the same with care through drunkenness, shall, upon due proof thereof, be liable to the penalties imposed by this act." Inn-keepers were to exhibit a copy of this act in their bar rooms.

140

WILLIAM MACTAVISH, 1815-1870

Governor Mactavish to the Inhabitants of Red River Settlement...16 November 1869.

[Fort Garry?, Man.: Printed at the office of the Nor'-Wester, Red River Settlement?, 1869].

This proclamation was issued by the governor of Assiniboia and Hudson Bay Company employee, William Mactavish, during the Red River Rebellion led by Louis Riel. By this proclamation, Mactavish transferred Rupert's Land to Canada. He was imprisoned by Riel shortly after.

141

FRANCIS BOND HEAD, 1793-1875. LIEUTENANT-GOVERNOR (1836-1838)

Proclamation: Reward: By Command of His Excellency the Lieutenant Governor: A Reward Is Hereby Offered, of Five Hundred Pounds, to Any One Who Will Apprehend and Deliver Up to Justice, Charles Duncombe...16th December, 1837.

[Toronto]: R. Stanton, [1837].

Reward broadside for the capture of Charles Duncombe and Robert Alway, reform members for Oxford; Finlay and

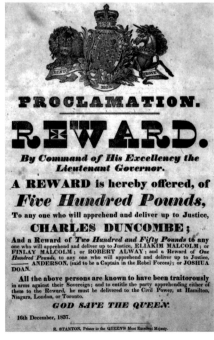

141   Proclamation: Reward: By Command of His Excellency the Lieutenant Governor.

142   *Proclamation! Whereas, the Honorable Thomas D'Arcy McGee, ...Was Foully Assassinated in This City...*

143   *Sir, Encouraged by the Advice of Some Friends, I Am Induced to Offer Myself as Candidate for the Clerkship to the House of Assembly...*

Eliakim Malcolm, of the "Western Rising" in the London District; as well as Joshua Doan. Duncombe and Eliakim Malcolm escaped to the United States; Finlay Malcolm and Alway were jailed briefly; and Joshua Doan was executed on February 6, 1839 in London, Upper Canada.

142

HENRY JAMES FRIEL, 1823-1869. MAYOR OF OTTAWA

Proclamation! Whereas, the Honorable Thomas D'Arcy McGee, ...Was Foully Assassinated in This City, on the Morning of the Seventh Day of April, 1868, ... I, Henry James Friel, Mayor of the City of Ottawa, Do Hereby Offer a Reward of $2,000 for the Apprehension and Prosecution to Conviction of the Assassin...

[Ottawa]: Bell & Woodburn, [1868].

This proclamation would have been posted in all public buildings and would have been read on that day by most citizens of the city of Ottawa.

143

WILLIAM LINDSAY, CIRCA 1761-1834

Sir, Encouraged by the Advice of Some Friends, I Am Induced to Offer Myself as Candidate for the Clerkship to the House of Assembly...

[Quebec: Samuel Neilson, 1792].

An early example of a printed circular letter. This one, sent by William Lindsay to Member of Parliament John Young,

was designed to solicit votes for the position of clerk of the House of Assembly.

144

Aux électeurs de la Basse-ville de Québec: messieurs et concitoyens: après la dissolution de notre Parliament provincial...

[Quebec: J. Neilson, 1796].

List of names supporting the candidacy of Augustin-Jérôme Raby (1745-1822) as member of Parliament for Lower-Town in Quebec City for the legislative election of 1796. Both Raby and John Young (circa 1759-1819), an influential merchant and politician, were elected in this second election in Quebec history.

145

The City of Toronto Poll Book. Exhibiting a Classified List of Voters, at the Late Great Contest for Responsible Government.

Toronto: Lesslie Brothers, 1841. 22 [2] p.

Before 1874, there was no secret ballot and citizens voted publicly for the candidate of their choice – when they were not intimidated to do otherwise. This poll book shows the names of voters listed by profession and the candidate they supported. This first election after the union of Upper and Lower Canada was one of the most violent in the history of Canada.

146   *Oxford Ratepayers! Look Out!*

147   *To the Electors of the South Riding of Oxford.*

146

Oxford Ratepayers! Look Out! You Are Called Upon Again to Vote Another £25,000 Tax. A Taxpayer, Ingersoll, June 30th, 1853.

Ingersoll: J. & J. Blackburn, 1853.

The taxes were being collected to finance the Grand Trunk Railway line between Montreal and Toronto.

147

S. RICHARDS

To the Electors of the South Riding of Oxford.

[Brantford?, Ont.]: Herald Cheap Job Press, [1861].

The message of this Liberal candidate reflected the main issues of the time: grants to the Grand Trunk Railway; the union of Lower and Upper Canada; and the early discussions of a federal union of all provinces.

148

ABRAM WILLIAM LAUDER, 1834-1884

Do thaghadairean na hearran mu dheas do shiorramachd Grey.

Toronto: Bell & Co., [1867].

Address to the electors of the county of Grey by A.W. Lauder, soliciting votes in the upcoming election. Lauder was elected to the Ontario Legislature in the riding of Grey South in September 1867.

149

West Durham Election!: Final Close of Polls, Right Triumphant! Blake & M'Leod Elected with Immense Majorities...

[Hamilton?, Ont., 1882?].

Broadside probably referring to the electoral victory of Edward Blake (1833-1912) during the 1882 or 1887 election. Prime minister of Ontario in 1871, Blake was leader of the federal Liberal Party from 1878 to 1887.

150

SPENCER ARGYLE BEDFORD, B. 1852

Contra Facts for the Electors of Moosomin District: Mr. C.B. Slater's Crowning Falsehoods, Mendacious Statements and Election Bunkum!: Mr. Slater's Single-Handed Game of Bluff.

Moosomin [Sask.]: T. Beer, [1885].

Broadside for an election held on September 15, 1885, to select a representative from Moosomin to sit on the Northwest Council. A rather unsubtle verbal attack on a political rival.

151

CONSERVATIVE PARTY (CANADA)

Free Traders, Attention!: The Following Is an Exact Copy of a Fly-Sheet Now Being Widely Circulated in Ontario by the Reform Party to Catch Protectionist Votes...

[S.l., 1887 or 1891?].

The "Reform party" was the Liberal party led by Wilfrid Laurier from 1887. The Liberal party supported free-trade with the United States while the Conservative party favoured protectionism. The latter, led by John A. MacDonald, won the elections in 1882, 1887, and 1891.

152

A gedanken vegen elekshen am 7ten november, 1900.

[Some thoughts about the election of November 7, 1900.]

Montreal: A.L. Kaplansky, 1900.

This Yiddish electoral supplement urges whole-hearted support for Sir Wilfrid Laurier's Liberal candidates. It had been inserted into the English language *Jewish Times*.

סיר ווילפריער לאוריער.

פרעמיער מיניסטער פֿאן קאנאדא, דער פֿירער פֿון דיא ליבעראלישע נאטירנעסמענט.

152 A gedanken vegen elekshen am 7ten november, 1900.

153

THE NATIONAL LIBERAL AND CONSERVATIVE PARTY AND PUBLICITY BUREAU

Women Voters Stop and Think!

Ottawa: Mortimer Co. Ltd., [1921]. 2 p.

The 1921 election was the first federal election in which women could apply the right to vote, which they had achieved in 1918. This pamphlet, favouring Arthur Meighen's policies, is asking women voters to think (and vote) for themselves.

154

PARTI LIBÉRAL

Liberal Rally Will Be Held at High School Mansonville, P.Q., Wednesday Afternoon at 1.30, October 17, 1923 / Assemblée libérale sera tenue à High School Mansonville, P.Q., mercredi après-midi à 1.30, octobre 17, 1923.

[Quebec (Province), 1923].

With a list of speakers including some ministers.

WOMEN VOTERS
Stop and Think!

• • •

Do you take opinions ready-made from some one else or do you form them for yourself? Would you wear a Fedora hat just because your father, husband, brother or son wears such headgear?

NO, of course you would not, you buy and wear something that suits yourself.

You USE YOUR OWN MIND in deciding what is best for you.

• • •

Are you employing the same principle when IT COMES TO CASTING YOUR BALLOT? Do you say "My father or husband is a Liberal or Conservative and has always voted for this party and I must do likewise?"

OR

Do you say "There is a vital issue to be decided on December 6th. I must cast my vote for the good of Canada? I must decide from the platforms presented what is the best for my country."

• • •

If you are a Thinking Woman, you will follow the Second Method. (OVER)

153 Women Voters Stop and Think!

Newspapers and Magazines

Feuilleton Extraordinaire.

L'AVENIR,

MONTREAL, Samedi soir, 18 Mars, 1848.

Grandes nouvelles

REVOLUTION EN FRANCE.

Le *Cambria* parti de Liverpool le 27 Février est arrivé et a apporté des nouvelles très importantes qui nous ont été communiquées par le télégraphe de Troy. Une révolution vint d'éclater en France. Louis-Philippe, a été détrôné, et le Comte de Paris a été proclamé roi de France. Les chemins de fer conduisant à Paris, ont tous été coupés afin d'arrêter toutes communications, et le peuple les a en son pouvoir. Louis-Philippe et la famille royale sont rendus en Angleterre. Nous avons dit plus haut que le Comte de Paris avait été proclamé roi, selon d'autres rapports, on a proclamé la république. Le sang a coulé à Paris et la garde nationale s'étant déclarée en faveur du peuple, le Palais des Tuileries a été saccagé. En Angleterre, on s'attendait de jour en jour à la formation d'un nouveau ministère. Nous aurons de plus amples détails à donner dans notre prochaine feuille.

L'élection de Terrebonne est fixée à lundi le 3 Avril prochain et celle de Montréal, à Mardi le 28 courant.

Often the first recorded printing by early Canadian printers, newspapers were weeklies sold by subscription – 200 to 300 at most – and carried more foreign than local news, official government notices, and a few advertisements. Many were short-lived, as were the early magazines which were unable to compete with the established and well-illustrated ones from England and the United States. It was not until the growth of the railroad and the increase in commercial activity that newspapers became dailies. The railroad distributed them to a wide area and up-to-date news could be received the same day by a greater number of readers. Paid advertising, rather than subscriptions, soon became what made newspapers profitable.

Magazines developed as Canadians acquired more leisure time. It was not until the 20th century that mass-produced Canadian magazines began to compete with their American counterpart.

This section of the exhibition is designed to show how early news travelled and to give only a few examples of 19th-century newspapers and magazines. The topic could have easily taken up the entire exhibition.

155

The Nova-Scotia Magazine and Comprehensive Review of Literature, Politics and News.

Halifax: John Howe, 1789-1792.

Founded by Reverend William Cochran in July 1789, the *Nova Scotia Magazine* is the earliest magazine published in Canada. John Howe, the father of Joseph Howe, both edited and printed it from June 1790. It was a monthly publication available by subscription – with an average of 200 subscribers – and made up mostly of articles and pieces of literature taken from foreign publications. The space given to local news and original contributions was very small and the readership soon declined.

156

Le Canadien.

Québec, 1806-1893.

157

The Quebec Mercury.

Québec, 1805-1863.

The first two truly political newspapers printed in Canada. The *Quebec Mercury*, founded by Thomas Cary, represented the interests of the English merchants, while the *Canadien* was the defender of the aspirations of the professional class of French Canadians. Obviously the two newspapers went head to head on numerous issues. This continued for a number of years and had a great influence on the events to come.

158

The Literary Garland.

Montreal: John Lovell: Lovell & Gibson, 1838-1851.

An important literary magazine, with such contributors as Charles Sangster, Susanna Moodie and Catherine Parr Traill, the *Literary Garland* was often illustrated with lithographs and was the first magazine to publish musical scores. It was also the first periodical to survive for more than three years.

159*

Le Foyer canadien. Recueil littéraire et historique.

Québec, 1863-1866. January-February, 1863 issue.

One of the leading literary periodicals of the "patriotic school" in French Canada, the *Foyer canadien*, claiming 2 000 subscribers, was begun by a group issued from *Les Soirées*

* This item not included in the exhibition.

canadiennes. A number of important literary and historical works were published in this periodical. Since a number of its contributors were employed by the government, the end of this periodical was brought about by the move in 1866-67 of the national capital to Ottawa.

160*

The Family Herald and Weekly Star.

Montreal, 1897-1956.

The most popular weekly in the rural parts of Canada.

161

Saturday Night.

Toronto, 1887-

Founded by Edmund Ernest Sheppard (1855-1920), *Saturday Night*, with its mixture of political criticism, international and national news, travel information, not to mention its literary supplement – which began in 1925 – was read by many generations of Canadians.

162

The Canadian Illustrated News.

Montreal, 1869-1883.

163

L'Opinion publique.

Montréal, 1870-1883.

Son of George Pascal Desbarats, Queen's printer and publisher of the *Foyer canadien*, George Edward Desbarats (1838-1893) resuscitated Alexander Sommerville's *Canadian Illustrated News*, which had been published in Hamilton between 1862 and 1864. Modeled on the *Illustrated London News*, *Harper's Weekly* and *L'Illustration*, the *Canadian Illustrated News* put the emphasis on illustrations using wood-engraving but also the leggotype, the new process of reproducing photographs devised by William Augustus Leggo of Montreal. In the first issue (October 30, 1869), Notman's portrait of Prince Arthur became the first photographic half-tone to appear in the history of journalism. Although its French-language equivalent, *L'Opinion publique* used many of the same illustrations, it remained a separate entity with its own writers and editorial staff. Of the many illustrators used by Desbarats, Henri Julien (1852-1908) is certainly the most famous. The thousands of illustrations found in these periodicals are one of the main sources for the iconography of the period.

164

WILLIAM BROWN, CIRCA 1737-1789 AND THOMAS GILMORE, D. 1773

Quebeck: To the Publick / Quebeck: au public.

[Philadelphia: William Dunlap?, 1763 or 1764].

The prospectus of the *Quebec Gazette / Gazette de Québec* was probably printed in William Dunlap's Philadelphia shop where William Brown and Thomas Gilmore worked. It was brought to Quebec and distributed by Brown, while his partner went to England to purchase equipment for their printing office. The first issue of the newspaper, the first in Quebec, appeared on June 21, 1764.

165

The Times. Le Cours du temps. 1794-1795.

Quebec: New Printing Office, February 1795.

An extraordinary reproducing the text of a letter from Noah Webster, dated Albany, February 2, 1795, and announcing the signing of Jay's Treaty on November 19, 1794.

The news appeared in the British papers, a copy of which was sent on board a ship from Bristol to New York. The ship probably arrived in the middle of January. On January 29, the news was conveyed in a letter by Webster to Albany where it was printed on February 2. A copy was sent to Quebec, arriving between two regular issues of the *Times*, February 2 and 9. The editor, William Vondenvelden (1753?-1809), judging it an important piece of news, did not wait for the next regular issue (Feb. 9), and had it printed as an extraordinary and sent to his subscribers.

Extraordinary: An item published by a newspaper in-between regular issues. Usually produced during wartime, it contains an announcement or information deemed sufficiently important or time sensitive to warrant immediate publication.

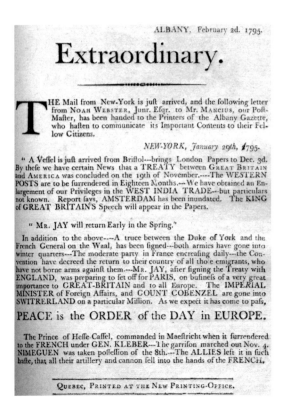

165 The Times. Le Cours du temps.

MORE GLORIOUS.

Herald Office, half past three, Tuesday, August 25.

MR. NEILSON,

We have not time to publish an Extra, but an express has just arrived from *General Brock*, with advices, that on the 15th inst. *General Hull* surrendered, with 2,500 men, 25 pieces of cannon, and all his stores, to the British arms, without the loss of a man on our side. This is all that has transpired, as the dispatches are just gone off to His Excellency, who is at present at the Camp. We congratulate you on this truly glorious news in great haste, and we are very sincerely,

Your most obdt. Servts.
The Editors of the Herald.

THURSDAY MORNING, 27th August, 1812.

Office du Herald à Montréal, 3½ heures après midi, Mardi 25 Août.

MR. NEILSON,

Nous n'avons pas le tems de publier un Extraordinaire ; un exprès vient d'arriver du Général *Brock*, avec la nouvelle que le 15 du courant le Général *Hull* s'est rendu avec 2500 hommes et 25 pièces de canons, et tous ses magasins, sans la perte d'un seul homme de notre côté. C'est tout ce qui est encore public. Les Dépêches viennent d'être envoyées à Son Excellence qui est au Camp. Nous vous félicitons sur cette grande et glorieuse nouvelle.

Les Redacteurs du Herald

166   More Glorious.

166

QUEBEC GAZETTE

More Glorious.

[Quebec: John Neilson, 1812].

This is John Neilson's printing of a message sent to him by the editors of the *Montreal Herald*, advising him that on August 25, 1812 they had received a "general order" announcing that General Brock had taken the Fort at Detroit.

167

L'Avenir. (1847-1858). Feuilleton extraordinaire.

Montréal, samedi soir, 18 mars 1848.

This is an interesting example of the progress of a major news story, the 1848 Revolution in France. "The *Cambria* which left Liverpool on February 27 has arrived and carries very important news which was sent to us by telegraph from Troy. A revolution has broken out in France..." [translation]. Indeed, steamer *Cambria* left Liverpool on February 27, 1848 and arrived in Halifax on March 15, and then in New York on March 18. It was thanks to the telegraph that this Montreal newspaper received the news from New York state the same day.

167   L'Avenir.

168

Le Pays. Montréal, 1852-1871.

Bulletin de jeudi, Montréal 26 mai 1870: dernières nouvelles de la frontière: mouvements féniens!

[Montreal, 1870].

Example of live reporting, hour by hour, of the battles of the Canadian troops against the Fenians at Frelighsburg and Cook Corners. The arrest of General O'Neil is also recorded in detail.

169

The Maple Leaf.

[Caen, France], 27 July 1944 - September 1944.

This newspaper was printed for Canadian soldiers in Caen (France) from July 27, 1944 to September 1944, and subsequently printed in Brussels until September 1945. Another edition had been printed in Italy beginning in January 1944. The ration was limited to one copy per seven soldiers.

Leisure and Literature

At the beginning of the last century, leisure time was very limited for most Canadians. Imported by British and Scottish immigrants, traditional sports, such as curling and cricket, were practised by officers of army garrisons and well-to-do citizens who organized their activities around clubs. By mid-century, factory owners and merchants were obliged to make the working day shorter, liberating evenings and Saturday afternoons for sporting activities. Enjoyed by all, friendly competitions occurred during association or company outings. Recreational activities such as cycling, rowing, and skating were encouraged by the development of manufactured equipment and the opening of new facilities. Canadians also began to develop their own sports such as lacrosse.

The opening of railway lines allowed teams to travel and leagues were formed. As sporting activities became more organized, rule-books and instruction manuals were printed locally. The appearance of professional sports, and by the same token, spectator sports, gave rise to a very active market for statistical manuals and programs directed at the fans.

Hobbies such as stamp and coin collecting also had their own specialized publications. Of course, reading of works of fiction had always been a favourite means of relaxation. Early Canadian novels were printed by subscription and limited to a few readers. Cheaper imported books far outweighed local productions and it was only at the beginning of this century that a few Canadian writers began to enjoy a large audience. During this century, Canadian-printed pulp magazines, comic books and popular novels did compete with the American market for certain periods of time.

170

WILLIAM GEORGE BEERS, 1843-1900

Lacrosse, the National Game of Canada.

Montreal: Dawson Brothers, 1869. xvi, 256 p.

This is the first book written on this sport in Canada. W.G. Beers, one of the most famous dentists of his time, was also the main codifier and promoter of the sport of lacrosse in Canada. This publication also shows the beginning of the use of photography – in this case William Notman's – as a mean of illustration.

170 Lacrosse, the National Game of Canada.
(See colour insert p. iii).

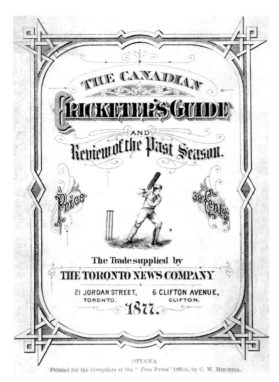

171   The Canadian Cricketer's Guide and Review of the Past Season.

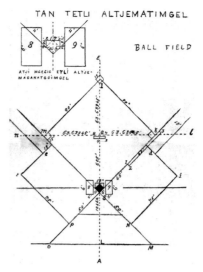

173   Altjematimgeoel. Spalding's Baseball Rules in Micmac.

171

T.D. PHILLIPPS, B. 1833 AND H.J. CAMPBELL

The Canadian Cricketer's Guide and Review of the Past Season.

Ottawa: Printed for the compilers at the Free Press Office by C.W. Mitchell, 1877. 136 p.

Cricket was played as early as the 1820s, mainly by garrison soldiers. From Confederation to the end of the 19th century, and even with the rise in popularity of baseball and lacrosse, cricket was the most popular summer sport in Canada and was played in all parts of the country.

172

JAMES BICKET

The Canadian Curler's Manual; or, An Account of Curling, as Practised in Canada: With Remarks on the History of the Game.

Toronto: Published at the office of the British Colonist for the Toronto Curling Club, 1840. 40, [1] p.

Although the first curling club was formed in Montreal by a group of Scotsmen as early as 1807, the sport only became popular in the 1830s. By the 1850s it had become very popular and was played by all classes of society. The author was secretary of the Toronto Curling Club.

173

Altjematimgeoel. Spalding's Baseball Rules in Micmac.

Rimouski, Québec.: Imprimerie générale S. Vachon, 1912. 31, [1] p.

Baseball was, at the time, one of the most popular outdoor sports in Canada, particularly in the regions situated close

to the United States. Shown here are the rules of baseball or balle-au-camp written in the Micmac language. One can see from the advertisement at the end, that this pamphlet was mainly distributed in New Brunswick where Micmac baseball teams were numerous.

174

ERNEST COMTE, ED.

Bottin officiel de baseball. Édition 1933.

Montréal: L'Association provinciale de Baseball, [1933]. 85 p.

American professional baseball was very popular, but this publication is mainly devoted to semi-professional and amateur teams in Quebec.

174 a   Bottin officiel de baseball. Édition 1933.

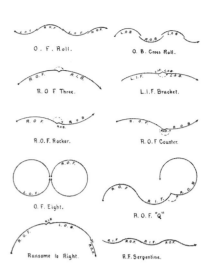

174 b *Bottin officiel de baseball. Édition 1933.*

175 *Skating: Hints for Beginners from the Experience of a Beginner.*

175

MINTO SKATING CLUB

Skating: Hints for Beginners from the Experience of a Beginner.

Ottawa: [The Club, 1906?]. [8] p.

The Minto Skating Club was founded in 1904 under the auspices of Lord and Lady Minto who also donated several trophies to the sport.

176

SWEET CAPORAL

Guide des ligues majeures de hockey. 1939-40. Première édition.

[Montreal?], 1939. 101 p.

These guides allowed the fans to have all the statistics on the players of the National Hockey League.

177

WILLIAM NORRIE ROBERTSON, B. 1855

Cycling!

Stratford [Ont.]: F. Pratt, 1894. 309, [43] p.

Certainly one of the first Canadian books on the bicycle. It contains a wealth of information on the appropriate costume to wear, training, tools, etc., along with a list of cycling champions.

178

Mrs. Redon's Benefit.

[Montreal: H.H. Cunningham, 1812].

Although a few circuses performed in Canada in the late 18th century, this is the oldest known circus broadside to be printed in Canada. It features the Pépin and Breschard

176 *Guide des ligues majeures de hockey.* (*See colour insert p. iv*).

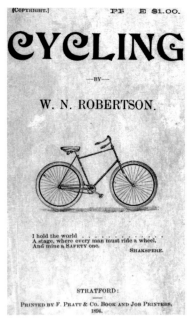

177 Cycling!

178 Mrs. Redon's Benefit.

circus, part of which, led by Cayetano Mariotini, toured eastern Canada. It gave performances in Montreal during the winter and spring of 1812 – including this one on March 12. It is an elaborate broadside for the times, using red ink and numerous type-faces to attract the attention of the passer-by.

179

SOCIÉTÉ SAINT-JEAN-BAPTISTE DE MONTRÉAL

Association Saint Jean-Baptiste, 1850: programme de la procession de lundi, 24 juin.

[Montreal]: Imprimerie de la Minerve, [1850].

A superb example of the use of different typefaces.

180

Town Hall: Mr. Youmans' Farewell Concert on Tuesday Evening, November 7th.

Stratford [Ont.]: Beacon Steam Print., 1876.

While general admission was 25 cents, "crying and crowing babies" were charged $1.00!

181

Dominion Day Celebration, Bayfield, Wednesday, July 1
[1896].

[Clinton, Ont.]: Clinton New Era Press, 1896.

Activities in these Dominion Day celebrations included football and baseball matches, as well as rowing and sailing. Prizes were awarded to encourage the competitors.

179 Association Saint Jean-Baptiste, 1850: programme de la procession de lundi, 24 juin.

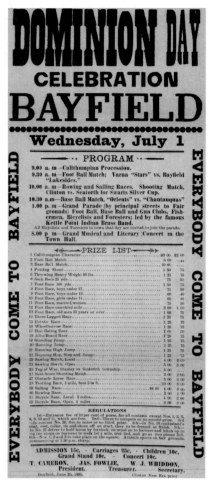

181 *Dominion Day Celebration, Bayfield...*

182 *Événement extraordinaire.*

182

Événement extraordinaire: grand course sensationnelle, dimanche 4 juillet 1909 à St. Celestin, au rond des courses du club, à 3 1/2 hrs. p.m.: cheval de M. Pental Vincent et Beaudet, le fameux coureur de fond de Victoriaville.

Victoriaville [Quebec]: Imp. l'Écho des Bois-Francs, [1909].

These races involving a man against a horse had been made popular by the famous runner nicknamed "Alexis le Trotteur."

183

GEORGE STEWART, 1848-1906

The Stamp Collector's Monthly Gazette.

St. John, N.B., [1865-1867].

One of the first philatelic periodicals to be published in British North America. George Stewart Jr. edited this periodical when he was only 16 years of age. The *Stamp Collector's Monthly Gazette* also included political commentaries and poetry. Stewart enjoyed a long career as journalist, editor and writer.

184

PIERRE NAPOLÉON BRETON, 1858-1917

Histoire illustrée des monnaies et jetons du Canada... / Illustrated History of Coins and Tokens Relating to Canada...

Montreal: P.N. Breton, 1894. 239 p.

One of the great coin dealers in Canada, P.N. Breton established a numerical system of classification for Canadian tokens which is still in use today.

185*

HENRY NAPOLÉON GRENIER, FL. 1864-1880

Leçons de photographie: description de procédés simples et faciles au moyen desquels on obtient presque infailliblement des épreuves sur papier.

Montréal: En vente chez tous les principaux libraires, 1864. 27 p.

The author was an artist-photographer in Montreal.

186

Lottery for Building a Prison, for the Town and District of Montreal / Lotterie [sic] pour bâtir des [sic] prisons, pour la ville & district de Montréal.

[Montreal: F. Mesplet, 1783].

* This item is not included in the exhibition.

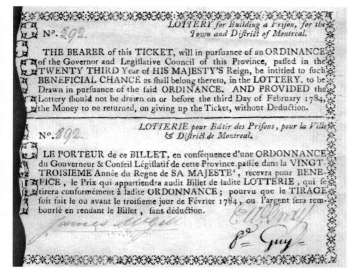

186   Lottery for Building a Prison, for the Town and District of Montreal.

Lottery ticket signed by James McGill (1744-1813), Edward William Gray (1742-1810) and Pierre Guy (1738-1812). Following an ordinance by the governor and legislative council, a lottery was organized to raise funds for the construction of a prison in Montreal.

187

ROYAL NEW BRUNSWICK LOTTERY

Grand Single Number Drawing: Royal New Brunswick Cash Distribution Will Take Place at St. Stephen, N.B., Canada, on the 15th April 1884.

[St. Stephen?, N.B.: W.D. Simpson & Co., 1884].

Broadside announcing a lottery in New Brunswick with a grand prize of $50 000 and a total of prizes of $128 500. Shown here is an unsold ticket of 50 cents for the draw of April 15, 1884. "There is at least one chance in every man's life to secure a fortune; this may be yours." Doesn't this remind you of a current slogan?

188

MADAME DE GOMEZ, 1684-1770

Histoire de Jean de Calais, roi de [sic] Portugal ou La vertu recompensee.

Québec, 1810. 72 p.

One of the few Canadian reprints of a work of popular French literature. This *Histoire de Jean de Calais* had been published during the 18th century in the "Bibliothèque bleue de Troyes," a famous collection of "dime novels."

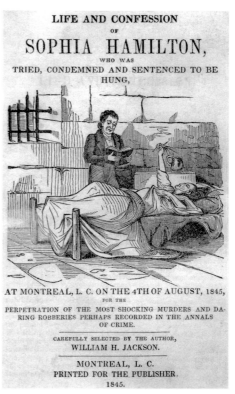

189   Life and Confession of Sophia Hamilton.

189

WILLIAM H. JACKSON

Life and Confession of Sophia Hamilton, Who Was Tried, Condemned, and Sentenced to Be Hung, at Montreal, L.C., on the 4th of August, 1845, for the Perpetration of the Most Shocking Murders and Daring Robberies Perhaps Recorded in the Annals of Crime.

Montreal: Printed for the publisher, 1845. 31 p.

Lives of criminals and descriptions of public executions were always popular with the public, and continue to be well into the 20th century.

190

WALTER BATES, 1760-1842

The Mysterious Stranger; or, The Adventures of Henry More Smith...

Charlottetown [P.E.I.]: Haszard & Owen, 1855. 109 p.

Walter Bates, a Loyalist who emigrated to Nova Scotia – the part which became New Brunswick – was high sheriff of Kings County. The recipe for a bestseller was there: the type of thief one would have enjoyed meeting, and the writing ability of Bates. First published in New Haven (Connecticut) and London (England) in 1817, this work was reprinted until 1910 and sold thousands of copies.

191*

JEAN BADREUX

Les Trois Crimes: Rawdon, St-Canut, St-Liboire: Histoire complète des meurtres, détails horribles, la vindicte publique.

Montréal: Leprohon & Leprohon, [1898]. 45 p.

192

Factual Detective Stories. (1941-1950).

Toronto: Norman Book Company. Vol. 4, no. 16. January 1945.

193

ADAM KIDD, 1802-1831

The Huron Chief, and Other Poems.

Montreal: Office of the *Herald* and *New Gazette*, 1830. 216 p.

Adam Kidd claimed he had sold 1 500 copies by subscription, quite a feat for the times. This copy bears the following inscriptions: "Theodosia Dunbar her book the gift of Mr. Robert Stuart" and "Miss. E. McDonell – In memory of me – J.M." These inscriptions connect the copy with the fur trade since Robert Stuart was a member of the Pacific Fur Company, and John McDonell (1768-1850) was a member of the North West Company and lived near Ottawa in Prescott and Pointe-Fortune.

193 The Huron Chief, and Other Poems.

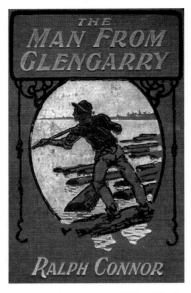

194 The Man from Glengarry: A Tale of the Ottawa.
(See colour insert p. iv).

194

RALPH CONNOR, PSEUD. OF CHARLES WILLIAM GORDON, 1860-1937

The Man from Glengarry: A Tale of the Ottawa.

Toronto: Westminster, 1901. 473 p.

Under the pen name of Ralph Connor, Charles William Gordon, a Presbyterian minister, was the most popular Canadian novelist of the beginning of the 20th century. His first three western novels, *Black Rock* (1898) and the two shown here, were classic melodramatic and edifying adventure stories, and sold a total of 5 million copies, an amazing success.

195*

RALPH CONNOR, PSEUD. OF CHARLES WILLIAM GORDON, 1860-1937

The Sky Pilot: A Tale of the Foothills.

Toronto: Westminster, 1899. 300 p.

196

LUCY MAUD MONTGOMERY, 1874-1942

Anne of Green Gables...

Illustrated by M.A. and W.A.J. Claus.

Boston: L.C. Page, 1908. viii, 429 p.

1st edition. 1st impression. April 1908.

Even though most of the early editions were published in the United States or Great Britain, *Anne of Green Gables* was always, and still is, an extremely popular novel with Canadian readers.

* This item is not included in the exhibition.

Petit Chaperon Rouge, entendant la grosse voix du loup, eut pour.

[17]

6
Little Folks Alphabet.
Toronto: Canada Games Co., [©1919]. [10] p.

8
Le Petit Chaperon Rouge
Montréal: Librairie générale canadienne,
[circa 1940]. 24 p.

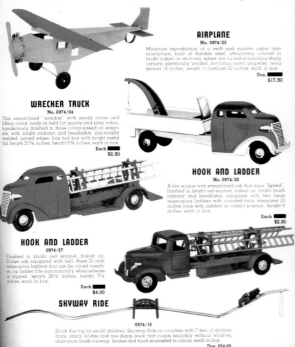

TURNER STEEL PULL TOYS

True-to-Life Reproductions Made of Auto Body Sheet Steel Finished in Excellent Quality Baked on Lustrous Bright Colored Enamels. Built to Resist the Wear and Tear of Hard Play.

AIRPLANE
No. 0974/23

Miniature reproduction of a swift and modern cabin type monoplane, built of durable steel, attractively colored in bright baked on enamels, edges are turned eliminating sharp corners, electrically welded, revolving metal propeller, wing spread 18 inches, length of fuselage 20 inches, each in box.
Doz. $17.50

WRECKER TRUCK
No. 0974/34

This streamlined "wrecker" with sturdy crane and lifting crank leads its field for quality and play value, handsomely finished in three colors baked on enamels, with bright radiator and headlights, electrically welded, turned edges, has tool box with bright metal lid, length 21¼ inches, height 8½ inches, each in box.
Each $2.80

HOOK AND LADDER
No. 0974/28

A fire wagon with streamlined cab that says "Speed", finished in bright red enamel, baked on, bright finish radiator and headlights, equipped with two large telescoping ladders with rounded rails, measures 22 inches long with ladders in correct position, height 6 inches, each in box.
Each $2.80

HOOK AND LADDER
0974/27

Finished in bright red enamel, baked on, Dodge cab equipped with bell, three 21-inch telescoping ladders that can be joined together, top ladder lifts automatically when release is tripped, length 28½ inches, height 7½ inches, each in box.
Each $4.00

SKYWAY RIDE
0974/15

Stock this toy for small children. Skyway Ride is complete with 7 feet of skyway track, stand, bridge and one dump truck that coasts smoothly without winding, aluminum finish runway, bridge and truck enameled in colors, each in box.
Doz. $24.00

95
Catalogue No. 87: Season 1939-1940.
Toronto: The Company, 1939. 224 p.

MOTHER SEIGEL'S

ALMANAC
1889

A. Sabiston & Co. Lith. Montreal.

234
Mother Seigel's Almanac. 1889.
[Montreal: A.J. White & Co., 1888].

TIME TABLE
Connections

GRAND TRUNK R. R.
Collingwood, Wiarton, Penetang, and Midland.

CANADIAN PACIFIC R. R.
Owen Sound, Algoma Mills and Sault Ste. Marie.

C. P. R. STEAMERS.
Sault Ste. Marie to Port Arthur.

STEAMER TELEGRAM,
Sault Ste. Marie, up North Shore Lake Superior to Otter Head.

MINN., ST. PAUL & S.S.M. R.
Sault Ste. Marie, to Minneapolis, St. Paul and the West.

ARNOLD LINE.
Mackinac, Cheboygan, St. Ignace.

L. M. & L. S. TRAN. CO.
Sault Ste. Marie, South Shore Lake Superior to Duluth Sault Ste. Marie, Milwaukee and Chicago.

MUSKOKA NAV. CO.
Rosseau and Port Cockburn for Muskoka Lakes, via. Parry Sound.

HART'S STEAMBOAT LINE
Mackinac Island, to Manistique, Escanaba and Green Bay.

ERIE AND WEST'RN TRANSPORTATION CO.
Sault Ste. Marie, Detroit, Cleveland and Buffalo.

NIAGARA NAV. CO.
Toronto to Niagara, Ont., and Lewiston, N.Y.

TIME TABLE
Excursion Fares

Route 1   Collingwood, Meaford, Owen Sound and Wiarton to Sault Ste. Marie and the Island of Mackinac, calling at Intermediate Ports on the North Shore and Manitoulin Island. Return Fare, meals and cabin berth included. ONLY $14.00

Route 2   Same trip as above from Toronto, Hamilton, Guelph, Stratford, Chatham, St. Thomas, and intermediate stations west to London. Return Fare, meals and cabin berth included. ONLY $18.50

Route 3   Collingwood, Penetang, or Midland to Parry Sound, Pointe Aux Barils, Byng Inlet, French River and Killarney. Return Fare, meals and cabin berth included. ONLY $6.00

Route 4   Same trip as above, from Toronto, Hamilton, Chatham, Guelph, Stratford, St. Thomas, stations west to London, via. Collingwood; Whitby, Peterboro' and Port Hope, via. Midland. Return Fare, meals and cabin berth included. ONLY $10.50

Route 5   Penetang, or Midland to Parry Sound, stopping at Minnecaug, Indian Harbor, Starvation Bay, Sans Souci and Parry Harbor. Return Fare, including meals. $4.50

Route 6   Same trip as above, from Toronto, Hamilton, Chatham, Guelph, Stratford, St. Thomas, Peterboro', Whitby, Port Hope and intermediate stations west to London. Return Fare ONLY including meals. $9.00

ALL TIME is subject to fluctuations by stress of weather or other causes.

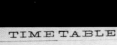

CABIN PLAN OF STEAMERS ON SAULT STE. MARIE & MACKINAC ROUTE:

STEAMERS CITY OF COLLINGWOOD AND CITY OF MIDLAND

PURCHASE YOUR TICKETS AND SHIP YOUR FREIGHT

Via. North Shore Nav. Co., of Ont., Ltd.—Black Line

Running in close connection with the G. T. R. and C. P. R. Companies. For Information, Freight Rates and Tickets, apply to any Agent of above Companies, or to

MAITLAND & RIXON, Agents, OWEN SOUND   M. BURTON, MANAGER, COLLINGWOOD

1894—SEASON—1894

POCKET
TIME TABLE
OF THE

NORTH SHORE
NAVIGATION CO.
OF ONTARIO, LTD.

GEORGIAN BAY
Royal Mail Line
—TO—
SAULT S. MARIE, MACKINAC, PARRY SOUND & FRENCH RIVER

STEAMERS
CITY OF COLLINGWOOD
NEW CITY OF MIDLAND
FAVORITE and MANITOU

LIGHTED WITH ELECTRICITY THROUGHOUT INCLUDING STATEROOMS, AND THE HIGHEST CLASSED IN LLOYD'S ON FRESH WATER

POPULAR BLACK LINE

M. BURTON, MANAGER,
COLLINGWOOD, ONT.

COLLINGWOOD ENTERPRISE PRINT

60

Lacrosse, the National Game of Canada.
Montreal: Dawson Brothers, 1869. xvi, 256 p

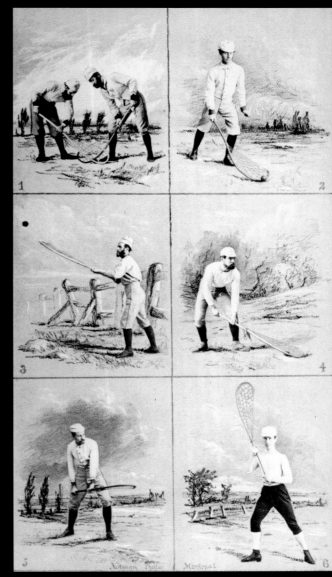

59
From Niagara to the Sea!
Montreal, 1901 (printed in Buffalo, N.Y.).

206
Commando Comics. [from circa 1942 to 1946].
Toronto: Bell Features. No. 7, [circa 1942-1943].

194
The Man from Glengarry: A Tale of the Ottawa.
Toronto: Westminster, 1901. 473 p.

176
Guide des ligues majeures de hockey. 1939-40.
Première édition. [Montreal?], 1939. 101 p.

97
Illustrated Price List for 1890.
London, Ont.: R. Southam, 1890. 159 p.

Séparateurs à crème standard.
Renfrew, Ont.: [Printed in Ottawa by Lowe-Martin, circa 1914].

198
Le Bracelet de fer. Grand roman canadien inédit. Ill.
d'Albert Fournier.
Montréal: Éditions E. Garand, 1926. 128 p.

211
Daring Confessions. (1942-1948?).
Toronto: Daring Publishing Co. Vol. 1, no. 1. March 1942.

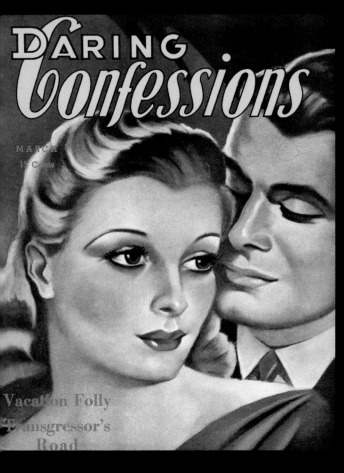

203
Last Night I Dreamed You Kissed Me.
Toronto: Leo Feist, [circa 1928] 6 p.

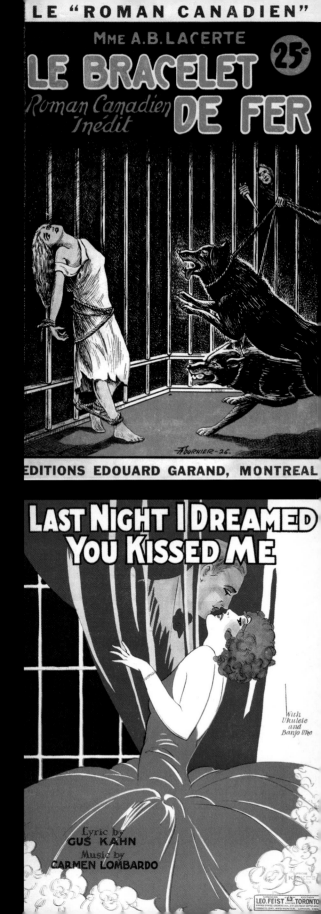

197

JEAN FÉRON, 1881-1946

La Prise de Montréal. Roman canadien inédit. Ill.
d'Albert Fournier.

Montréal: Éditions E. Garand, 1928. 76 p.

Publisher Édouard Garand (1901-1965) was very successful with the 79 titles of the series "Le Roman canadien," of
which 35 were written by Jean Féron, a farmer from
Saskatchewan, nicknamed "the Canadian Alexandre
Dumas." With an illustrated cover, and historical and
melodramatic themes, these books were quite popular.
The use of newsprint and a text on two columns allowed
Garand to sell these novels at a very low price making
them accessible to a large audience.

198

ADÈLE BOURGEOIS LACERTE, 1870-1935

Le Bracelet de fer. Grand roman canadien inédit. Ill.
d'Albert Fournier.

Montréal: Éditions E. Garand, 1926. 128 p.

199

THÉODORE FRÉDÉRIC MOLT, 1795-1856

**Elementary Treatise on Music: More Particularly
Adapted to the Piano Forte / Traité élémentaire de
musique: particulièrement adapté au piano forté.**

Quebec: Neilson & Cowan, 1828. 69, ix p. and engraved music.

The first bilingual work of musical instruction published in
Canada. The author used a series of conversations
between the master and the student. The music scores at
the end of the book were engraved on copper.

Copy belonging to Eulalie-Antoinette Dénéchaud, wife
of Marc-Pascal de Sales Laterrière, who gave it to Louise
de Sales Laterrière, probably her daughter. Ms. Dénéchaud
added her red morocco book-plate on the first cover of the
book. This is a good example of a music book which was
probably found in all well-to-do and educated families in
Lower Canada.

200

LESLIE STUART

The Soldiers of the Queen.

Toronto: The Anglo Canadian Music Publishers Association, Ltd.,
[circa 1898]. 6 p.

A very popular song of the Boer War. A note on the cover
of this copy indicates a printing run of 1 500 copies distributed between three publishers.

198 Le Bracelet de fer. (See colour insert p. vi).

201

ERNEST LAVIGNE, 1851-1909

Laissez-moi dormir!

Montréal: Lavigne et Lajoie, [circa 1880]. 3 p.

Brilliant musician, composer and bandmaster, Lavigne
entered the music publishing trade in 1877 and entered
into a partnership with Louis-Joseph Lajoie in 1881. He is
best remembered as the founder of Sohmer Park in
Montreal.

201 Laissez-moi dormir!

202
GORDON V. THOMPSON
I Want to Kiss Daddy Good Night.

Toronto: Thompson Publishing Co., [circa 1916]. 4 p.

One of the popular songs of World War I.

203
CARMEN LOMBARDO (1903-1971) AND GUS KAHN
Last Night I Dreamed You Kissed Me.

Toronto: Leo. Feist., [circa 1928]. 6 p.

The music of Carmen Lombardo, Guy Lombardo and his band of Royal Canadians was always very popular even after they moved to the United States.

204*
HENRY DEYGLUN
Vie de famille.

Montréal: Éd. Archambault, [circa 1939]. 4 p.

Melody inspired by the radio-novel by Henry Deglun who also wrote the lyrics.

205
CHARLES-ÉMILE GADBOIS
La Bonne Chanson. Septième album.

[Saint-Hyacinthe?, circa 1946].

A collection of the most popular songs in French Canada.

203   *Last Night I Dreamed You Kissed Me.*
(See colour insert p. vi).

206   *Commando Comics.*
(See colour insert p. iv).

Before World War II, Canadians read comic books and pulp magazines which were imported from the United States. The War Exchange Conservation Act of December 1940 restricted the importation of non-essential commodities from the United States, including comic books. This gave Canadian publishers a captive market, and the first regular format Canadian comic book, *Better Comics (No. 1)*, was published in March 1941 in Vancouver by Maple Leaf Publishing. After the war, Canadian comics again had to compete with foreign publications. Beginning in 1948, there was a growing concern from parents and the general public that crime comic books and crime pulp magazines were a contributing factor in leading young people into criminal activities. Crimes by children who were avid readers of comic books fuelled the campaign to have them banned. Bill 10, which became known as the Fulton Bill after MP Davie Fulton, became law on December 10, 1949. It made it an offence to make, print, publish, distribute, sell, or own "any magazine, periodical or book which exclusively or substantially comprises matter depicting pictorially the commission of crimes, real or fictitious." Non-crime comic books survived and have enjoyed fluctuating popularity both in French and English Canada.

206

Commando Comics. [from circa 1942 to 1946].

Toronto: Bell Features. No. 7, [circa 1942-1943].

This war series specialized in showing military heroics by Canadian soldiers.

* This item is not included in the exhibition.

207
Hérauts. Le Trésor de la jeunesse. (1944-1965).
Paris: Fides. 3e année, numéro 17. 20 mai 1952.

Printed in Canada but published by the Paris branch of Fides from 1944 to 1965, *Hérauts* first used text which was translated from the American. Later, most of the content was Canadian, and it even used Canadian artists. The material was mainly religious and historical in nature, and designed to edify rather than amuse. It was distributed through the school system to thousands of students for over 20 years. By the mid 1960s, it could not compete with publications from France such as *Tintin* and *Spirou*.

208
Wow Comics. (1941-1946).
Toronto: Commercial Signs of Canada, and later Bell Features. Issue no. 1 (September 1941).

This issue was the first Canadian colour comic book. Fifty thousand copies were printed.

209
Cerebus the Aardvark. (December 1977 to the present).
Kitchener, Ont.: Aardvark-Vanaheim. Vol. 1, no. 33 (December, 1981).

The longest running Canadian comic book.

210
Croc. (October 1977 to the present).
Montréal: Ludcom Inc. N°. 72 (July 1985).

The most popular humour magazine, which includes some comic strips, in French Canada with an astonishing 75 000 copies printed.

211
Daring Confessions. (1942-1948?).
Toronto: Daring Publishing Co. Vol. 1, no. 1. March 1942.

Example of early Canadian pulp magazines.

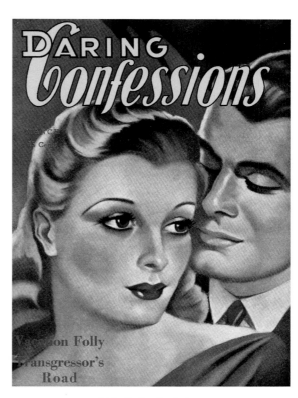

211 *Daring Confessions.*
(See colour insert p. vi).

Religion

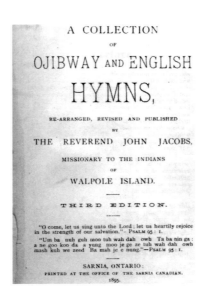

Religion played a vital role in the lives of all early Canadians. A bible could probably be found in all Protestant homes and a catechism in most Roman Catholic ones. Because of the size of bibles, it was much cheaper to import them than to print them locally. The smaller catechism, on the other hand, had a long printing history in Quebec.

Canadian printing of other religious books took the form of hymn-books, sermons, lives of saints, reprints of foreign publications, and numerous translations into the various Native languages. Each religious movement had its newspaper which often had more subscribers than many of the popular dailies.

The catechism is the work which teaches Catholics what they should know and do in order to lead a Christian life. It must be precise, clear and accessible to all, especially to children. Throughout the history of French Canada, it is, with the almanac, the most common book to be found in the home. It is the equivalent of the Bible for Protestants. The first catechism printed in Canada is the *Catéchisme du diocèse de Sens*. Two editions were printed by Brown and Gilmore in Quebec in 1765 and 1766 (see the section entitled Book-Object). The second is the *Catéchisme à l'usage du diocèse de Québec*, written by Bishop Jean-Olivier Briand, and printed in Montreal by Fleury Mesplet in 1777. The first official catechism written by a Canadian-born priest, Bishop Joseph-Octave Plessis, was *Le Petit Catéchisme du diocèse de Québec* published in 1815. Many modifications were incorporated in these works during the next 150 years.

212

MGR JEAN-OLIVIER BRIAND, 1715-1794

Catéchisme à l'usage du diocèse de Québec.

Saint Philippe, Québec: Impr. ecclésiastique, 1825. 84 p.

Although Bishop Briand's catechism was no longer approved by the religious authorities after 1815, father François-Xavier Pigeon (1778-1838), printer in Saint-Philippe, put out two editions, in 1825 and 1827.

Copy from the collections of Victor Morin and G.-A. Daviault.

213

MGR JOSEPH-OCTAVE PLESSIS, 1763-1825

Le Petit Catéchisme du diocèse de Québec. Nouv. éd. approuvée et autorisée.

Montréal: Imprimé par Rolland & Thompson, 1845. 71 p.

The first official catechism written by a native Canadian.

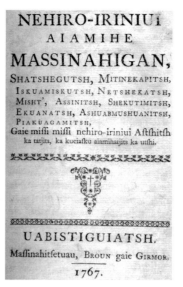

216 *Nehiro-iriniui aiamihe massinahigan...*

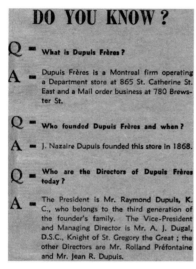

214 *The Catechism of the Ecclesiastical Provinces of Quebec, Montreal and Ottawa...*

216

JEAN-BAPTISTE DE LA BROSSE, 1724-1782

Nehiro-iriniui aiamihe massinahigan, Shatshegutsh, Mitinekapitsh, ...

Uabistiguiatsh [Quebec]: Massinahitsetuau, Broun gaie Girmor [Brown and Gilmore], 1767. 96 p.

> Prayer book in the Montagnais language. It is the first full-length book in a Native language printed in Canada, and one of the few used in Canada during the 18th century.

217

JOHN JACOBS

A Collection of Ojibway and English Hymns Re-arranged, Revised and Published by the Reverend John Jacobs, Missionary to the Indians of Walpole Island. Third edition.

Sarnia, Ont.: Printed at the office of the Sarnia Canadian, 1895. v, 488 p.

214

The Catechism of the Ecclesiastical Provinces of Quebec, Montreal and Ottawa... Translated from the French. New edition.

Quebec, 1945. xiv, 103 p.

> English translation of this catechism "of compromise" which was used from 1888 to 1950. This copy was bound and distributed by the large French-language retail store Dupuis Frères which made sure to include an English-language ad inside the covers

215*

Catéchisme catholique. Édition canadienne.

Québec, 1953. 287 p.

> The catechism of "modern times."

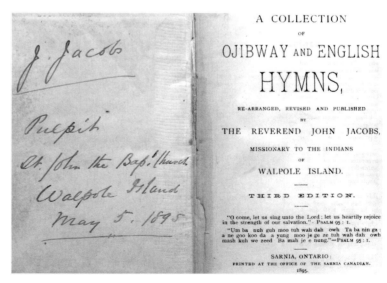

217 *A Collection of Ojibway and English Hymns.*

* This item is not included in the exhibition.

The author's copy with this note: "J. Jacob. Pulpit, St. John the Bapt. Church Walpole Island, May 5, 1895." Walpole Island reservation is situated at the mouth of the St. Clair River in Ontario.

218

CHURCH OF ENGLAND

The Book of Common Prayer, and Administration of the Sacraments...According to the Use of the Church of England.

Toronto: General Board of Religious Education, [circa 1940]. 299 p.

One of the late religious imprints by the Church of England in Cree. The text is in syllabic characters with roman letters on facing pages.

219

L'Office de la Semaine sainte, selon le messel & breviaire romain.

Montreal: F. Mesplet & C. Berger, 1778. 420 p.

Copy of Marguerite Cartier (1793-1878), sister of Sir Georges-Étienne Cartier.

220

JÉRÔME DE GONNELIEU, 1640-1715

L'Imitation de Jésus-Christ. Traduction nouvelle avec une pratique et une prière à la fin de chaque chapitre. Nouvelle édition.

Québec: Imprimé à la Nouvelle-Imprimerie, 1813. xxi, 543 p.

Copy with manuscript notes on the flyleaf which give the names of the previous owners, all of the same family:

219   *L'Office de la Semaine sainte, selon le messel & breviaire romain.*

François Dugas in 1815, then his son Edouard Dugas (died in 1868), his son Father Georges Dugas (1833-1928), clerc de Saint-Viateur who gave it to his Order in 1915.

221

Neuvaine à l'honneur de St. François Xavier.

Nouvelle édition.

Montréal: James Lane, 1817. 118 p.

The first edition had been printed in Montreal by Fleury Mesplet in 1778. The very small size of these works permitted worshippers to carry them everywhere. The following inscriptions allow us to trace its many owners: "Josette Latrimouille, Montréal, 4 mars 1828"; "Marie-Claire Daveluy arrière petite-nièce de Mesdames Josette et Sophie Latrémouille. Montréal mai 1914"; and "Present from my sister Josette Latrémouille. Montreal, May 5 1829, Sophie Campbell."

222*

Petit manuel des cérémonies romaines, à l'usage du diocèse de Québec.

Québec: Fréchette et Cie., 1832 . iv, 278 p.

Handbook designed to help altar boys and other persons assisting the priest during the religious services. These books were used long after their date of publication. This copy was owned in 1862 by Louis Baril, of Gentilly, 30 years after the initial publication.

223

ANDREW FULLER, 1754-1815

The Gospel Worthy of All Acceptation, ... New edition.
With a Life of the Author.

Charlotte-Town, P.E.I.: J.D. Haszard, 1833. xxxii, 196 p.

Copy of George Truman of Amherst [Nova Scotia].

224

AMOS BLANCHARD, 1801?-1869

Book of Martyrs; or, A History of the Lives, Sufferings, and Triumphant Deaths of the Primitive and Protestant Martyrs: From the Introduction of Christianity, to the Latest Periods of Pagan, Popish, Protestant, and Infidel Persecutions. 10th ed.

Kingston, U[pper] C[anada]: Published by Blackstone, Ellis and Graves, 1835. 540 p.

Anti-Catholic propaganda work by an American writer. Edition printed in Cincinnati, but with the imprint of a Kingston publisher.

* This item is not included in the exhibition.

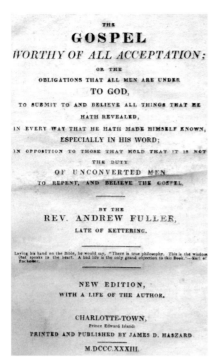

223 The Gospel Worthy of All Acceptation...

224 Book of Martyrs.

225

A Selection of Psalms, Hymns and Anthems, for Every Sunday and Principal Festival throughout the Year.

Toronto: Printed at the Diocesan Press, H. & W. Rowsell, 1842. 244 p.

Copy belonging to Charles Reid, Hamilton, October 14, 1844.

226

CHARLES STEWART, 1775-1837

Two Sermons on Family Prayer: With Extracts from Various Authors, and a Collection of Prayers.

Montreal: Nahum Mower, 1814. 394 p.

The author was minister of the parish of Saint-Armand in Quebec and later became bishop of Quebec. In 1809, Stewart built the first Anglican church in the Eastern Townships at Frelighsburg. "To provide a focus for spiritual study during his absences, he [Stewart] had a number of his sermons printed from 1810 to 1814, hundreds of copies of which were distributed freely" (*Dictionary of Canadian Biography*, vol. VII, p. 826). Copy which belonged to Pliny Moore in 1825, then to Sophia Whiteside in 1829, and later to Margaret Robertson Whiteside Wilbor, April 19, 1860.

227

The Doctrines and Discipline of the Methodist Episcopal Church in Canada.

York [Toronto]: Published by E. Ryerson and F. Metcalf, 1829. 162 p.

This book was probably purchased by James Rosamond (1805-1894) shortly after he arrived in Carleton Place in 1830 from Ireland. He entered the textile business and operated the first known textile mill in the eastern half of the province from 1846 to 1857. He then moved his business to Almonte. The book was eventually passed on to J. Mackintosh Bell (1877-1934), geologist, explorer, soldier and writer who was related to the Rosamonds through his mother.

228

Translations and Paraphrases, in Verse, of Several Passages of Sacred Scripture Collected and Prepared by a Committee of the General Assembly of the Church of Scotland, in Order to Be Sung in Churches.

Halifax, N.S.: Reprinted by J. Howe, 1790. 68 p.

At the end of the 18th century, most of the basic religious works were imported from Europe, but, in some cases, they were reprinted by the first Canadian printers. Copy owned by Elizabeth Perkins, née Young (with her signature dated 1813). She was the wife of famous merchant and writer, Simeon Perkins (1735-1812), mainly known for his journal published by the Champlain Society.

229

The Mason's Manual: Comprising Rules and Regulations for the Government of the Most Ancient and Honorable Society of Free and Accepted Masons, in Lower-Canada.

Quebec: Printed at the New Printing-Office by T. Cary, Junr. & Co., 1818. vi, 114, [4] p.

This manual, which all members where encouraged to purchase, had been written by a committee of the Grand Lodge of the City of Quebec. This copy was owned in 1818 by St. George's Lodge No. 16, in Trois-Rivières.

230

DUGALD BUCHANAN, 1716-1768

Laoidhean spioradail [bound with] **Dain spioradail le Paruig Grannd.**

Montreal: J. Starke & Co., 1836. 72 , 175, 50 p.

A rare Montreal imprint in Welsh. Copy with this note: "Cathrine M. Diarmid's Hymn Book. October 10th 1836" and "To John Christie, Genesee [Alberta] near Slabcity a present from his niece Mrs. M. Diarmid, April 16th 1839."

231*

The Christian Guardian.

Toronto, 1829-1925.

Founded by Egerton Ryerson, the *Christian Guardian*, a Methodist newspaper, became the most popular church paper before Confederation with an estimated readership in 1832 of 3 000.

230   *Laoidhean spioradail.*

---

* This item is not included in the exhibition.

Health

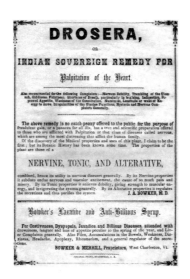

Since there were few doctors to serve a widespread population, most Canadians relied on home remedies and care. Many almanacs carried recipes designed to cure almost anything, and, in the later years, advertisements for a variety of miracle products.

The medical history of countries is often one of a series of epidemics and Canada is no exception. Typhus, cholera, venereal disease, and tuberculosis had outbursts throughout Canadian history and gave rise to numerous publications for their prevention and cure.

Although announcements of births and marriages are rather late occurrences in the printing history in this country, funeral notices were printed by most of the 18th-century Canadian printers.

232

**An Almanack for the Year of Our Lord, 1811, ...:
Calculated for the Meridian of Halifax, in Nova-Scotia.**

Halifax: Printed and sold by John Howe & Son, [1810].

Much information on the activities of early Canadian doctors has reached us through the almanacs they used as agendas. This copy belonged to well-known doctor William Bruce Almond (1787-1840) of Halifax. He has written up a list of persons vaccinated in 1810 and 1811 – probably against typhus – which included Judge Haliburton and his son, the future author of *The Clockmaker*. It was the son of the printer of this almanac, Joseph Howe, who published *The Clockmaker* in 1838. In June 1840, Dr. Almond contracted typhus after attending to passengers of a ship moored in Halifax, and died a few weeks later.

233

DAVIS & LAWRENCE (MONTREAL)

Pain Killer Calendar and Cookery Book.

[Montreal?], 1886.

Certain almanacs were published by distributors of pharmaceutical products. One finds advertisements for different products such as, in this case, the Perry Davis Pain Killer, "reputed" treatment against cholera – which continued to claim victims – mixed in with kitchen recipes. This ad boasts of the effectiveness of bear grease for the hair. This copy has the stamp of Dr. G.W. Prentiss of Grenville (Quebec).

234

Mother Seigel's Almanac. 1889.

[Montreal: A.J. White & Co., 1888].

This almanac advertises Mother Siegel's syrup, pills and ointment, and contains letters from satisfied customers written from different parts of Canada. One suspects that the same letters were updated over the years. This copy was distributed by Dr. G.W. Prentiss of Grenville (Quebec). It has attractive lithographed wrappers, and shows the string with which the almanac could be attached to a prominent place in the kitchen.

235*

Dodd's Almanac. 1943. Useful Information for Family and Home.

[Toronto]: The Dodds Medecine Co. Ltd., [1942].

This is the same type of advertising almanac, but this time for Dodd's kidney pills. It contains testimonials from different Canadians mixed with "medical information." This almanac was sent by mail to clients. Our original envelope is postmarked December 9, 1942.

* This item is not included in the exhibition.

234   *Mother Seigel's Almanac. 1889.*
(See colour insert p. ii).

236

Almanach du buveur pour 1907.

Rimouski, Québec: Imprimerie générale de Rimouski, [1906?].

The fight against intemperance was continuous, but intensified around the turn of the century. This almanac contains stories showing the dangers of alcohol, and reproduces drawings designed to show the harmful effects of alcoholism on the family. This publication was mainly distributed in the Gaspé area and on the North Shore.

236   *Almanach du buveur pour 1907.*

237

SAMUEL THOMSON, 1769-1843

New Guide to Health; or, Botanic Family Physician.

Brockville [Ont.]: Printed for W. Willes by W. Buell Jr. & Co., 1831. 192, 132 p.

During a certain period, works of popular medicine, breaking away from traditional medicine, were very popular in Canada. Samuel Thomson, an American, and his followers believed that sickness was mainly due to a loss of heat and treated their patients with remedies of vegetable origin such as cayenne pepper. But there was more than medicine in these first popular manuals published in Upper Canada. Thomson was also an ardent republican and conveyed his reformist beliefs in his works. It is not a coincidence that three editions of this work were published in Upper Canada by reform printers and distributed in all of southern Upper Canada on the eve of the 1837 Rebellion.

238

Home and Health and Compendium of Useful Knowledge: A Cyclopedia of Facts and Hints for All Departments of Home Life, Health, and Domestic Economy, and Hand Book of General Information.

London, Ont.: Advertiser Print. and Pub. Co., 1883. 346 p.

With the economic, technological and demographic developments of the end of the last century, there was a need to publish encyclopedic works gathering all knowledge useful to the family.

238   *Home and Health and Compendium of Useful Knowledge.*

239
EDOUARD MOREAU

Instructions sur l'art des accouchemens, pour les sages-femmes de la campagne.

Montréal: Impr. de Fabre, Perrault et Cie., 1834. 44 p.

The practice of home birth by mid-wives was so widespread that this work was approved by the Medical Bureau of Montreal.

240*
SHEILA KITZINGER

Homebirth: And Other Alternatives to Hospital.

Toronto: Macmillan of Canada, 1991. 208 p. Photographs by Marcia May.

A modern variation on the same theme.

241*
JOHANN GEORG ROSENSTEIN

The Comparative Merits of Alloeopathy, the Old Medical Practice, and Homoeopathy, the Reformed Medical Practice, Practically Illustrated.

Montreal: Rollo Campbell, 1846. viii, 287 p.

242*
AGNÈS SAINT-LAURENT

Guide pratique des remèdes naturels: des centaines de conseils santé.

Westmount, Québec: Sélection Reader's Digest, 1996. 334 p.

Very popular today, homeopathy was also practised in the middle of the 19th century.

243

The Domestic Physician and Traveller's Medical Companion / Compiled from the Practice of the Most Eminent Physicians and Surgeons, viz., Sir Astley Cooper, Sir Henry Halford... &c. &c. by a Physician.

Toronto: Eastwood & Skinner, 1838. 136 p.

As in this case, manuals of traditional medicine were mainly of British origin. In a note on the flyleaf, the previous owner had indicated who should inherit this copy. Its condition clearly shows the use that had been made of it.

244
BOWKER & MERRILL

Drosera, or Indian Sovereign Remedy for Palpitation of the Heart.

Stanstead [Canada East]: Journal Print, [circa 1845-1850].

As a centre of printing for southern Quebec, Stanstead was an ideal choice for firms from the northeastern states, in this case West Charleston, Vermont. Founded

244   Drosera, or Indian Sovereign Remedy for Palpitation of the Heart.

by Lee Roy Robinson, a journalist from Vermont, the *Stanstead Journal* printed many books, pamphlets, and did most of the job printing for this Anglophone enclave.

245
WOLFRED NELSON, 1791-1863

Practical Views on Cholera, and on the Sanitary, Preventive and Curative Measures to be Adopted in the Event of a Visitation of the Epidemic...

Montreal: B. Dawson, 1854. 19 p.

While he was mayor of Montreal, Wolfred Nelson, patriot of the Rebellion of 1837 and a famous doctor, published at his own expense, in French and in English, this small pamphlet for the prevention of cholera. This last epidemic, originating in the United States, raged from mid-June to mid-September 1854, and killed 5 000 people in British North America.

246

Rules to Be Observed by the Public for the Preservation of Health and the Speedy Cure of Cholera... J. Guthrie Scott, Sec.

Montreal: Montreal Board of Health, [circa 1854].

Broadside published by the Montreal Board of Health – established in 1851 – at the height of the 1854 cholera epidemic. Designed to aid in both the prevention and the cure of the disease, it recommended the consumption of certain foods, beverages and medicines, as well as directing citizens to relief depots.

This item is not included in the exhibition.

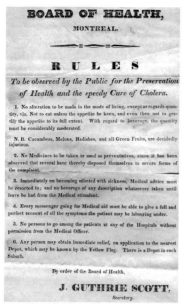

246 *Rules to Be Observed by the Public for the Preservation of Health...*

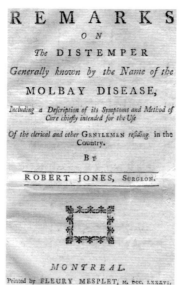

247 *Remarks on the Distemper Generally Known by the Name of the Molbay Disease.*

247

ROBERT JONES

Remarks on the Distemper Generally Known by the Name of the Molbay Disease: Including a Description of Its Symptoms and Method of Cure Chiefly Intended for the Use of the Clerical and Other Gentlemen Residing in the Country.

Montreal: Fleury Mesplet, 1786. 19, [1] p.

The "Mal de la Baie Saint-Paul" or "Molbay [*sic* for Malbaie] disease," which affected many people in this region, was considered by the majority of doctors, except the author of this pamphlet and a few others, as a venereal disease. One can notice that this pamphlet was designed to be distributed to a select part of the population, namely to the members of the clergy and "other gentlemen residing in the country."

248

Venereal Disease: What You Should Know: Every Canadian Citizen Must Help in Solving the Problem of Venereal Disease in Canada.

[Canada, circa 1940]. [4] p.

Mimeographed pamphlet with the text in Cree and in English.

249

SYLVANUS STALL, 1847-1915

What a Young Husband Ought to Know.

Philadelphia: The Vir Publishing Co.; Toronto: W. Briggs, 1897. 300 p.

A very popular series at the time, with numerous titles for young men, young women, young brides, etc. An "instruction" book on sexuality, marriage and parenthood.

250*

LIEUT. J.R. BYERS

Fighting Tuberculosis. Written for Canadian Soldiers Who Are Suffering from Lung Disease.

Ottawa: Military Hospitals Commission, [1916]. 24 p.

251

THE CANADIAN TUBERCULOSIS ASSOCIATION

What You Should Know about Tuberculosis.

Ottawa: F. A. Acland, 1923. 16 p.

The author was medical officer at the famous Ste. Agathe des Monts sanatorium in the Laurentians. Tuberculosis was one of the most common diseases of the beginning of the 20th century.

Funeral notices were usually printed on one half of a sheet, leaving the other half to write the name of the receiver, since most were mailed or delivered by hand. They were later illustrated with appropriate wood engravings and eventually with the photograph of the deceased.

252

[Notice for the funeral of William Ellice].

[Montreal: Fleury Mesplet, 1790].

Most probably a member of the well-known family of merchants.

253

[Notice for the funeral of Ms. Angélique Adhémar].

[Montreal: Eusèbe Senécal, 1864].

S I R,

T H E favour of your Company is requeſted at the Funeral of Mr. WILLIAM ELLICE deceaſed, on to morrow at 5 o'Clock P. M. from the houſe of Madam Waden.

Montréal, Tueſday 28 *September* 1790.

252 *Notice for the funeral of William Ellice.*

* This item is not included in the exhibition.

Book-Object

Bibliophiles and book collectors are well known as lovers of the book as an object. Few early Canadian book owners were bibliophiles, but since books were scarce and expensive, they were cared for, repaired, and passed on to the next generation.

The examples shown here demonstrate the many different ways in which copies were either transformed or personalized, and in other cases, how they were considered important enough to be taken as spoils of war or salvaged from a maritime disaster.

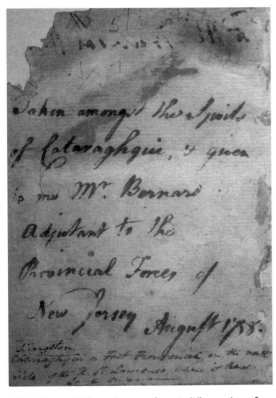

254   *Heures de Nostre-Dame en français: A l'usage des enfans.*

254

Heures de Nostre-Dame en français: A l'usage des enfans.

Bordeaux: Chez la veuve de J. De La Court..., 1748. 272 p.

This book was owned by a resident of Fort Frontenac (Fort Cataraqui) and was part of the spoils which the troops of Major Bradstreet took after the surrender of the fort in August 1758. A manuscript note on the flyleaf reads as follows: "Taken among the spoils of Cataraghqui, & given to me, Mr. Bernard, Adjutant to the Provincial Forces of New Jersey, August 1758."

255

JEAN-JOSEPH LANGUET, 1677-1753

Catechisme du diocese de Sens.

Quebec: Chez Brown & Gilmore, 1766. 148, [3] p.

Second Canadian edition of this important catechism. Copy from the library of Father Charles-Joseph Brassard Deschenaux (1751-1832), Catholic priest, seigneur, and important bibliophile whose library contained over 2 000 volumes. Books being quite scarce in Canada during the 18th century, it was common practice to make manuscript copies of certain popular books. After the printed catechism, Deschenaux had bound a manuscript – dated 1772 – of the *Cantiques spirituels sur les points les plus importans de la religion et de la morale chrétienne,* a work which had often been reprinted in France during the 18th century.

From the library of Victor Morin.

256

L'Office de la Semaine sainte et de celle de Pâque: En latin et en françois selon le missel et bréviaire romain.
Nouvelle édition.

Québec: Imprimé à la Nouvelle imprimerie, 1816. 575 p.

Contemporary red long-grained morocco binding, stamped with the name of Catherine-Louise Lovell, niece of seigneur Charles-Louis-Roch de Saint-Ours, and of Jacques Dorion (1797-1877), doctor and member of Parliament.

257

JAMES EVANS, 1801-1846 AND GEORGE HENRY, FL. 1837-1848

Nu-gu-mo-nun O-je-boa an-oad ge-ë-se-üu-ne-gu-noo-du-be-üng uoô Muun-gou-duuz gu-ea Moo-ge-gee-seg ge-ge-noo-ü-muu-ga-oe-ne-oug.

New York: Printed by D. Fanshaw, 1837. 392 p.

On October 16, 1839, the barque *Colborne*, sailing from London to Quebec City, sank at the mouth of Chaleur Bay. According to a note from Henry W. Baldwin, sheriff of Gloucester (New Brunswick), this copy was part of the cargo found on the beach after the tragedy. It belonged to Elizabeth Field (1804-1890), wife of Peter Jones (1802-1856), Sauteux chief and Methodist minister, and had her name on the front cover of the binding "Elizabeth Jones alias Geje-uguumeegoa." Fortunately she had returned from England on another ship.

258

JEAN-BAPTISTE BOUCHER-BELLEVILLE, 1763-1839

Recueil de cantiques à l'usage des missions, des retraites, et des catéchismes. Troisième édition.

Québec: John Neilson, 1800. 338 p.

Very popular work which saw four editions from 1795 to 1804. The original binding was "repaired" and rebacked using a piece of leather sewn to the covers. Pieces of metal were fixed to the outside of the covers: a "house" binding. Copy of Michel Dumont, Rivière du Loup, in 1804.

259

The Holy Bible, Containing the Old and New Testament...

London: George Eyre and Andrew Strahan, 1813.

In early Canada, most bibles were imported from England or the United States. This family bible belonged to Thomas Molson (1791-1863), second son of John Molson, Sr. (1763-1836), founder of the business enterprises. It was given to Thomas by his father and contains this inscription on the title-page "Donum ab meo patre [signed] Thomas Molson." The first two blank leaves contain the birth and death dates of children from 1817 to the death of Thomas' wife Martha Molson in 1848. Later inscriptions in pencil bring the list up to Thomas' own death in 1863.

260

Die gemeinschaftliche Liedersammlung, zum allgemeinen Gebrauch des wahren Gottesdienstes.

Berlin [Kitchener, Ont.]: Heinrich Eby, 1841. 395 p.

Calf binding with upper board extended into a curved flap fitting under a strap of the lower board. Copy belonging to Peter Eby with his lettered leather label on upper board and engraved bookplate: "Peter Eby, Drucker, Berlin, Wellington District, Canada West. August 24, 1844." Peter Eby, a son of bishop Benjamin Eby (1785-1853) and brother of printer Heinrich Eby, was the owner of several German-language newspapers during the 1850s and 1860s. A typical binding for a book designed to be carried in hand or lying flat, rather than being shelved.

260 *Die gemeinschaftliche Liedersammlung, zum allgemeinen Gebrauch des wahren Gottesdienstes.*

261

Form of Prayers for the Feast of New Year with English Translation. Revised edition.

New York: Hebrew Publishing Company.

During World War II, Jews with German or Austrian citizenship were placed in internment camps in Canada. Mr. Schessinger, interned in a camp at Ile-aux-Noix, was called to Farnham to lead High Holiday services. In gratitude, the Jewish camp community gave him this book with an inscription signed by Dr. Manfred Saalheimer and Heinz Abrahamson.

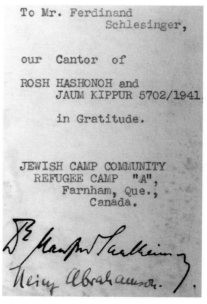

261 *Form of Prayers for the Feast of New Year with English Translation.*

References Consulted

Paul Aubin. *Le Manuel scolaire dans l'historiographie québécoise.* Sherbrooke: GRELQ, 1997.

Joyce Banks, comp. *Books in Native Languages in the Rare Book Collections of the National Library of Canada.* Revised and enlarged edition / *Livres en langues autochtones dans les collections de livres rares de la Bibliothèque nationale du Canada.* Édition revue et augmentée. Ottawa: National Library of Canada / Bibliothèque nationale du Canada, 1985.

John Bell, ed. *Canuck Comics: A Guide to Comic Books Published in Canada.* Montreal: Matric Books, 1986.

Jacques Bernier. *La Médecine au Québec: Naissance et évolution d'une profession.* Québec: Presses de l'Université Laval, 1989.

Bruno Bettelheim. *The Uses of Enchantment: The Meaning and Importance of Fairy Tales.* New York: Alfred A. Knopf, 1977.

Mary E. Bond. *Canadian Directories, 1790-1987: A Bibliography and Place-Name Index / Annuaires canadiens, 1790-1987: Une Bibliographie et un index des noms de lieux.* Ottawa: National Library of Canada / Bibliothèque nationale du Canada, 1989. 3 vols.

Raymond Brodeur et autres. *Les Catéchismes au Québec, 1702-1963.* Sainte-Foy [Quebec]: Presses de l'Université Laval, 1990.

J.M. Bumsted. *The Peoples of Canada.* Vol.1. *A Pre-Confederation History.* Vol.2. *A Post-Confederation History.* Toronto: Oxford University Press, 1992. 2 vols.

J.M. Bumsted. *Interpreting Canada's Past.* Second edition. Toronto: Oxford University Press, 1993. 2 vols.

Jennifer J. Connor and J.T.H. Connor. "Thomsonian Medical Literature and Reformist Discourse in Upper Canada" in *Canadian Literature,* no. 131 (winter 1991), p. 140-155.

Bryan Dewalt. *Technology and Canadian Printing: A History from Lead Type to Lasers.* Ottawa: National Museum of Science and Technology, 1995.

Dictionary of Canadian Biography / Dictionnaire biographique du Canada. Toronto: University of Toronto Press; Québec: Presses de l'Université Laval, 1966-

G.P. de T. Glazerbrook. *A History of Transportation in Canada.* Toronto: McClelland and Stewart, 1964. 2 vols.

J. Russell Harper. *Early Painters and Engravers in Canada.* Toronto: University of Toronto Press, 1981.

Denis Goulet et André Paradis. *Trois Siècles d'histoire médicale au Québec: Chronologie des institutions et des pratiques (1639-1939).* Montréal: VLB Éditeur, 1992.

Groupe de recherche sur l'édition littéraire au Québec (GRELQ). *L'Édition du livre populaire.* Sherbrooke: Les Éditions Ex Libris, 1988.

Historical Atlas of Canada / Atlas historique du Canada. Vol. 2. 1800-1891. Toronto: University of Toronto Press; Montréal: Presses de l'Université Laval, 1993.

Maxwell L. Howell and Reet A. Howell, eds. *History of Sport in Canada.* Revised edition. Champaign, Ill.: Stipes Publishing Co., 1985.

Jean-Jacques Jolois. *J.-F. Perrault (1753-1844) et les origines de l'enseignement laïque au Bas-Canada.* Montréal: Presses de l'Université de Montréal, 1969.

George L. Parker. *The Beginnings of the Book Trade in Canada.* Toronto: University of Toronto Press, 1985.

Paul Rutherford. *A Victorian Authority: The Daily Press in Late Nineteenth-Century Canada.* Toronto: University of Toronto Press, 1982.

S.E.D. Shortt, ed. *Medicine in Canadian Society: Historical Perspectives.* Montreal: McGill-Queen's University Press, 1981.

Fraser Sutherland. *The Monthly Epic: A History of Canadian Magazines, 1789-1989.* Markham, Ont.: Fitzhenry & Whiteside, 1989.

J. Donald Wilson, Robert M. Stamp and Louis-Philippe Audet, eds. *Canadian Education: A History.* Scarborough, Ont.: Prentice-Hall, 1970.

Appendices

APPENDIX A

DATE OF INTRODUCTION OF PRINTING IN A FEW CANADIAN CITIES

1751 - Halifax, Nova Scotia
1764 - Quebec City, Quebec
1776 - Montreal, Quebec
1783 - Saint John, New Brunswick
1783 - Shelburne, Nova Scotia
1787 - Charlottetown, Prince Edward Island
1793 - Niagara, Ontario
1798 - York [Toronto], Ontario
1807 - Saint John's, Newfoundland
1841 - Norway House, Manitoba
1858 - Victoria, British Columbia
1859 - Winnipeg, Manitoba
1860 - New Westminster, British Columbia
1880 - Edmonton, Alberta

APPENDIX B

POPULATION OF CANADA (Approx. figures in thousands)

	ca. 1791	ca. 1845	1851	1871	1901
Newfoundland	15	96	124[*]	147[**]	221[***]
New Brunswick	20	155	194	286	331
Nova Scotia	40	202	277	388	460
Prince Edward Island	6	47	63	94	103
Lower Canada [Quebec]	171	697	890	1192	1649
Upper Canada [Ontario]	–	432	952	1621	2183
Manitoba	–	–	–	25	255
Saskatchewan	–	–	–	–	91
Alberta	–	–	–	–	73
British Columbia	–	–	55	36	179
Yukon	–	–	–	–	27
North West Territories	–	–	5	48	20

[*] For the year 1857. *Encyclopedia of Newfoundland and Labrador.* 1981-
[**] For the year 1869. *Ibid.*
[***] For the year 1902. *Ibid.*

Modified from *Historical Statistics of Canada.* 2nd ed. 1983.

APPENDIX C

LITERACY RATES (% of population)

	1861 (over 20 yrs. old)	1871 (over 20 yrs. old)	1891 (over 20 yrs. old)	1901 (over 5 yrs. old)
Ontario	92.8	92.1	93.1	91.3
Quebec	64.1	64.1	70.4	82.3
Maritimes	77.4*	84.2	91.9	85.4
West	–	–	88.9	77.8
Canada as a whole	–	81.1	84.7	85.6

*Nova Scotia only
Modified from Paul Rutherford. *A Victorian Authority: The Daily Press in Late Nineteenth-Century Canada.* 1982.

Index

This index includes all the proper names of individuals and corporate bodies that appear in the bibliographic entry for each item.

A. & W. Mackinlay & Co. 36
A. & W. Mackinlay 34
A.C. Fortin 22
A.J. White & Co. 234
A.L. Kaplansky 152
Aardvark-Vanaheim 209
Achard, Eugène 8
Acland, F.A. 251
Advertiser Print. and Pub. Co. 238
Allen, W.H. 124
Almon, Mather Byles 121
Andrews, William Eusebius 25
Angers, Réal 127
Anglo Canadian Music Publishers Association, Ltd., The 200
Anthon Henrich 80
Archambault, Éd. 204
Association provinciale de Baseball, L' 174
Atelier typographique du "Canadien" 38
Augustin Germain 99
Avery 122
B. Dawson 245
Badreux, Jean 191
Baldwin, Cradock, and Joy..., 46
Barnett, George 90
Bas-Canada. Adjutant général des milices 130
Bates, Walter 190
Bayfield, Henry Wolsey 50
Beacon Steam Print. 180
Bedford, Spencer Argyle 150
Beer, T. 150
Beers, William George 170
Belisle, L.-A. 9
Bell & Co. 148
Bell & Woodburn 142
Bell Features 206, 208
Bicket, James 172
Blackburn, J. & J. 146
Blacklock, H., & Co. 52
Blackstone, Ellis and Graves 224
Blanchard, Amos 224
Bödecker und Stübing 4
Boisseau, Nicolas-Gaspard 129
Boucher-Belleville, Jean-Baptiste 258
Bouchette, Marie-Caroline-Alexandra [pseud. Maxine] 7
Boulanger, Roland 8
Bourne, George 69
Bouthillier, Jean Antoine 29
Bowker & Merrill 244
Boyd, John Alexander 37
Breton, P.N. 184
Breton, Pierre Napoléon 184
Briand, Mgr. Jean-Olivier 212
Briggs, G.C. 101
Briggs, W. 249
British American Land Company. Quebec Emigrant Agency Office 44
British Colonist Office 138
Broun gaie Girmor 216
Brown & Gilmore 255
Brown and Gilmore 216
Brown, William 164
Brown, William, and Thomas Gilmore 129
Brunswick Press 13
Bryce, W. 117
Buchanan, Alexander Carlisle, Sr. 48
Buchanan, Dugald 230
Buckton, C. 2
Buell, W., Jr. & Co. 237
Bushell, John 120
Byers, Lieut. J.R. 250
C. Buckton 2
C. Le François 17
C.W. Mitchell 171
Campbell, H.J. 171
Campbell, J. 37

Campbell, James, & Son 10, 109
Campbell, Rollo 241
Canada Food Board 103
Canada Games Co. 6
Canada. Department of National Revenue 54
Canada. Department of the Interior 53, 54
Canadian National Railways 64
Canadian Pacific Railway 52, 56
Canadian Tuberculosis Association, The 251
Caporal, Sweet 176
Carswell 84
Cary, T. 70
Cary, T., Ex typis 20
Cary, T., Junr. & Co. 229
Cary, Thomas, et Cie. 3
Cavelier, Guillaume, fils 16
Chubb, Henry, & Company 83, 112
Church of England 218
Clarke Printing Co. Ltd. 65
Claus, M.A. and M.A.J. 196
Clinton New Era Press 181
Coates, W.J. 89
Coffin, William Foster 133
Commercial Signs of Canada 208
Commissioners of National Education in Ireland, The 34
Committee of the General Assembly of the Church of Scotland 228
Compagnie J-B. Rolland & Fils 107
Comte, Ernest 174
Conservative party (Canada) 151
Cook & Fletcher 91
Cowan, W. 28
Cunnabell, J.S. 121
Cunningham, H.H. 178
Curry, W. 47
D. and J. Smillie 69
D. Fanshaw 257
Dalton, T. 89
Daly, Dominick 57
Daring Publishing Co. 211
Davis & Lawrence (Montreal) 233
Dawson Brothers 170
Dawson, B. 245
Day, B.H. 117
De Courtenay, J.M. 109
De La Court, J., Veuve de, ... 254
De Sola, Abraham 78
Demers, Jérôme 20
Derbishire, S., et G. Desbarats 131
Deyglun, Henry 204
Diocesan Press, H. & W. Rowsell 225
Dodds Medecine Co. Ltd., The 235
Doige, Thomas 86
Dougall, J., & Son 77
Doyle, Martin 47
Dunlap, William 164
E. Ryerson and F. Metcalf 227
Eastwood & Skinner 254
Eaton, T., Co. Limited, The 92, 93
Eby, Heinrich 260
Écho des Bois-Francs, Imp. l' 182
Éd. Archambault 204
Éditions A. Lévesque 7
Éditions E. Garand 197, 198
Élie, W. 128
Elzéar Vincent 50
Eusèbe Sénécal 253
Evans, James 257
Ex typis T. Cary 20
Eyre, George and Andrew Strahan 259
F. Mesplet & C. Berger 219
F. Mesplet 186
F. Pratt 177
F.A. Acland 251
Fabre, Perrault et Cie., Impr. de 239

Fanshaw, D. 257
Faribault, Marthe 14
Feist, Leo. 203
Féron, Jean 197
Fessenden, Arthur 118
Fides 207
Figler, I. 5
Fleury Mesplet 247, 252
Fortin, A.C. 22
Fréchette et Cie. 18, 127, 222
Fréchette et Cie., Imprimerie de 19
Friel, Henry James 142
Fuller, Andrew 223
G. Robinson 114
G.C. Briggs 101
Gadbois, Charles-Émile 205
Garand, E., Éditions 197, 198
Gazette Office 48
Gendron 9
General Board of Religious Education 218
George Eyre and Andrew Strahan 259
Gilmore, Thomas 164
Gleason, Thomas Henri 88
Gomez, Madame de 188
Gonnelieu, Jérôme de 220
Gordon, Charles William [pseud. Ralph Connor] 194, 195
Grand Trunk Railway Company of Canada 62
Grant, John Charles 115
Grenier, Henry Napoléon 185
Groundwood Books 15
Guillaume Cavelier fils 16
H. Blacklock & Co. 52
H. Ramsay 32, 33
H. Rose 62
H.C. Thomson 137
H.H. Cunningham 178
Hackstaff, George H. 72
Hall & Fairweather 122
Hamilton Bus Lines Ltd. 66
Haszard & Owen 190
Haszard, J.D. 30, 223
Haszard, James D., Royal Gazette Office 45
Head, Francis Bond 141
Heaton Publishing 11
Hebrew Publishing Company 85, 261
Heinrich Eby 260
Henry Chubb & Company 83, 112
Henry, George 257
Herald Cheap Job Press 147
Héritage 14
Holmes, Jean 21
Howard, Frederick P. 90
Howe, J. 228
Howe, John 155
Howe, John, & Son 51, 232
I. Figler 5
Ile de Vancouver 138
Imp. l'Écho des Bois-Francs 182
Impr. de Fabre, Perrault et Cie. 239
Impr. ecclésiastique 212
Imprimerie de Fréchette et Cie. 19
Imprimerie de la Minerve 179
Imprimerie générale de Rimouski 236
Imprimerie générale S. Vachon 173
Imprimerie J. Moronval 99
Iris Office, The 72
J. & J. Blackburn 146
J. Campbell 37
J. Dougall & Son 77
J. Howe 228
J. Lovell 35, 75
J. M'Coubrey 27
J. Millen 67
J. Neilson 29, 31, 81, 144
J. Potts, Herald Office 73
J. Starke & Co. 230
J. Starke 133
J. Wilkie 114
J.B. Thompson & Co. 34
J.D. Haszard 30, 223
J.S. Cunnabell 121
Jackson, William H. 189
Jacobs, John 217
James Campbell & Son 10, 109

James D. Haszard Royal Gazette Office 45
James Lane 86, 221
John Bushell 120
John Howe & Son 51, 232
John Howe 155
John Lovell 78, 158
John Millen & Son Ltd. 67
John Neilson 115, 116, 136, 166, 258
Jones, Robert 247
Journal Print 244
Kahn, Gus 203
Kaplansky, A.L. 152
Kidd, Adam 193
Kitzinger, Sheila 240
Knight, Nancy 11
L. Perrault 100
L.-A. Belisle 9
L.C. Page 196
L.P. Normand 40
La Brosse, Jean-Baptiste de 216
Lacerte, Adèle Bourgeois 198
Lambly, John 49
Lane, James 86, 221
Languet, Jean-Joseph 255
LaRoche, G. 119
Laroque, G. 110
Lauder, Abram William 148
Lauder, Sir Thomas Dick 112
Lavigne et Lajoie 201
Lavigne, Ernest 201
Le François, C. 17
Le Jeune, Jean-Marie Raphael 39
Légaré, P.T., Limitée 96
Lemay, J.-Arthur 7
Leo. Feist 203
Leprohon & Leprohon 191
Lequien, E.A. 28
Lesslie Brothers 145
Lesslie, R., & Sons 23
Levert, Mireille 14, 15
Lévesque, A., Éditions 7
Lewellin, John 45
Lhomond, C.F. 31
Librairie générale canadienne 8
Lindsay, William 143
Lombardo, Carmen 203
Lovell and Gibson 1, 87, 158
Lovell, J. 35, 75
Lovell, John 78, 158
Lowe, S. 12
Lowe-Martin 111
Lower Canada. Court of General Quarter Sessions of the Peace (District of Montréal) 58
Lower Canada. Court of King's Bench (District of Montreal) 135
Lower Canada. Legislature. House of Assembly 136
Ludcom Inc. 210
Lyons, Jacques Judah 78
M'Coubrey, J. 27
Mackay, Robert Walter Stuart 87
Mackinlay, A. & W. 34
Mackinlay, A. & W., & Co. 36
Macmillan of Canada 240
Mactavish, William 140
May, Marcia 240
McClary Manufacturing Co. 97
McKenzie, Mackay & Co. 125
McMullen, D. 24
Meilleur, Jean Baptiste 22
Menon 99
Mercier & Cie. 110
Mesplet, F. 186
Mesplet, F., & C. Berger 219
Mesplet, Fleury 247, 252
Methodist Episcopal Church in Canada, The 227
Middleton, Robert 76
Military Hospitals Commission 250
Millen, J. 67
Millen, John, & Son Ltd. 67
Miller, R. & A. 35, 106
Minto Skating Club 175
Missionary Press 79
Mitchell, C.W. 171
Molt, Théodore Frédéric 199
Montgomery, Lucy Maud 196
Montreal Board of Health 246
Moreau, Edouard 239
Moronval, J., Imprimerie 99
Mortimer Co. Ltd. 96, 153

Most Ancient and Honorable Society of Free and Accepted Masons, The 229
Mower, N. 25, 135
Mower, Nahum 118, 226
Murray, Lindley 23
N. Mower 25, 135
N. Thibault & G. LaRoche 119
Nahum Mower 118, 226
National Liberal and Conservative Party and Publicity Bureau, The 153
Neilson and Cowan 88, 199
Neilson, J. 29, 31, 81, 144
Neilson, John 115, 116, 136, 166, 258
Neilson, Samuel 143
Neilson, William 21
Nelson, Wolfred 245
Nerlich & Company 95
Nesbitt, Thomas T. 50
New Brunswick. Post Office 74
New Printing Office 49, 130, 165
Norfolk Messenger Office 139
Norman Book Company 192
Normand, L.P. 40
North American Transportation Co. Ltd., The 61
North Shore Navigation Company of Ontario Ltd. 60
Nouvelle-Imprimerie 130, 220, 256
Nova Scotia. Custom House (Halifax, N.S.) 120
Office of the British Colonist 172
Office of the British Columbian and Victoria Directory 90
Office of the Herald and New Gazette 193
Office of the Nor'-Wester, Red River Settlement 140
Office of the Sarnia Canadian 217
Ogilvie Flour Mills Company 102
P.N. Breton 184
P.T. Légaré Limitée 96
Page, L.C. 196
Parti Libéral 154
Perrault, Charles 8, 9
Perrault, Joseph François 17, 18, 19
Perrault, L. 100
Phillipps, T.D. 171
Picton Gazette Print 24
Plessis, Mgr. Joseph-Octave 213
Potts, J., Herald Office 73
Pratt, F. 177
Primrose 12
Quebec and Lake St. John Railway 63
Quebec Gazette 166
R. & A. Miller 35, 106
R. Lesslie & Sons 23
R. Southam 97
R. Stanton 141
Ramsay, H. 32, 33
Randall, Stephen 26
Renfrew Machinery Company Ltd., The 111
Rennie, William 108
Rennie's, W., Sons 108
Richards, S. 147
Richardson, John 114
Richelieu & Ontario Navigation Co. 59
Robert Middleton 76
Robert Simpson Company Limited, The 94
Robert Watson & Co. 123
Robertson, William Norrie 177
Robinson, G. 114
Rolland & Thompson 213
Rolland, J.B., & Fils, Compagnie 107
Rollo Campbell 241
Rose, H. 62
Rosenstein, Johann Georg 241
Roy, Jennet 32, 33
Royal New Brunswick Lottery 187
Russell, Peter 42
Ryerson, E., and F. Metcalf 227
S. Derbishire et G. Desbarats 131
S. Lowe 12

Saint-Laurent, Agnès 242
Samuel Neilson 143
Sangster, John Herbert 35
Scobie and Balfour 1
Scott, J. Guthrie 246
Sélection Reader's Digest 242
Sellen, H.E.M. 11
Sénécal, Eusèbe 253
Simpson, Robert, Company Limited, The 94
Simpson, W.D., & Co. 187
Sinclair 71
Singer Sewing Machine Company 98
Smillie, D. and J. 69
Smillie, D. and James 69
Smith, James 38
Smith, John 105
Société Saint-Jean-Baptiste de Montréal 179
Somerville 125
Southam, R. 97
Spalding 173
St. John, William Charles 27
Stall, Sylvanus 249
Stanton, R. 141
Starke, J. 133
Starke, J., & Co. 230
Stewart, Charles 226
Stewart, George 183
Stuart, Leslie 200
Suzor, Louis Timothée 131
T. Beer 150
T. Cary 70
T. Cary, Junr. & Co. 229
T. Dalton 89
T. Eaton Co. Limited, The 92, 93
Teuscher, Jakob 4
Theophrastus [pseud.] 51
Thibault, N. 119
Thibault, N., & G. LaRoche 119
Thomas Cary et Cie. 3
Thompson Publishing Co. 202
Thompson, Gordon V. 202
Thompson, J.B., & Co. 34
Thomson, H.C. 137
Thomson, Hugh Christopher 137
Thomson, Samuel 237
Townsend, J. Howard 134
Trans-Canada Air Lines 68
Upper Canada 139
Upper Canada. Executive Council 43
Upper-Canada Gazette office, The 82
Vachon, S., Imprimerie générale 173
Vancouver Island 138
Vancouver Island Coach Lines Ltd. 65
Veuve de J. De La Court... 254
Vincent, Elzéar 50
Vir Publishing Co., The 249
W. Briggs 249
W. Bryce 117
W. Buell Jr. & Co. 237
W. Cowan 28
W. Curry 47
W. Rennie's Sons 108
W.D. Simpson & Co. 187
W.J. Coates 89
Waddell, Rev. James 30
Walton & Gaylord 26, 104
Walton, George 89
Waters, William, and Titus G. Simons 42
Watson, Robert, & Co. 123
Westminster 194, 195
White, A.J., & Co. 234
Wilkie, J. 114
William Brown and Thomas Gilmore 129
William Dunlap 164
William Neilson 21
William Waters and Titus G. Simons 42
Wilson and Hyman 126
Witness Job Office 84